VILLAGES AT WAR

BACKWELL NAILSEA
TICKENHAM AND WRAXALL.
1939 - 1945

PETER WRIGHT

PETER WRIGHT
in association with
NAILSEA AND DISTRICT LOCAL HISTORY SOCIETY

FIRST PUBLISHED IN GREAT BRITAIN 1990 by
PETER WRIGHT IN ASSOCIATION WITH NAILSEA
AND DISTRICT LOCAL HISTORY SOCIETY
5 THE PERRINGS,
NAILSEA,
BRISTOL BS19 2YD

PETER WRIGHT ISBN 0 9516257 0 5
N & D LHS ISBN 0 9516258 0 2

CONTENTS

This book is dedicated to those people who lived in the four villages through the eventful years 1939-1945

GB 22 4 bc

Nur für den Dienstgebrauch

Bild Nr. 2450 Z 22

Aufnahme vom 29. 4. 42

Nailsea

Munitionslager

Länge (westl. Greenw.): 2° 46′ Nördl. Breite: 51° 27′

Zielhöhe über NN: 91 m

500 m 0 500 1000 m

Maßstab: 1:14500 i. Bildmitte

Lfl. Kdo. 3 Juli 1942

Karte 1:100000

GB/E 32

1. 7 Munitionshäuser
2. abgeholzte Flächen, anscheinend zum Bau weiterer Munitionshäuser bestimmt

VILLAGES AT WAR –

INTRODUCTION

Backwell, Nailsea, Tickenham and Wraxall lie in a cluster roughly eight miles to the south west of Bristol. Although there has been considerable residential development in the area, mainly in Nailsea, there are sufficient wartime inhabitants of the four villages who have been willing to help to try to tell the story of the four "parishes", which for convenience I have referred to as the 'Villages', during the 1939-1945 war.

From the mid 1870's, when the failure of the local coal mines ensured the total collapse of the Nailsea Glass industry and with it the end of a century or more of industrial development, the Villages had been settling down to an agricultural role. As 1939 approached changes were about to take place and there was to be an influx of new faces the like of which had not been seen before.

This story is told wherever possible in the words of those who lived in the villages during the war. If in using these I have taken them out of context and implied a different meaning the mistake is mine. Nearly all the photographs have been supplied by the contributors and while thanking them for allowing me to use them to illustrate this book I freely acknowledge their owners' copyright.

I have attempted to verify statements made to me but corrections or further information sent to me at the address given in the front of the book will be gratefully received.

This book could not have been produced without the assistance and encouragement of many of the members of Nailsea and District Local History Society and the forbearance of my wife and my colleagues at work who have commented on the drafts.

In particular I would like to thank Hilary Duncan who produced the original typescript from my handwritten notes, Julie Mainstone for the drawings and Debbie Pond and the team at Sun Life Creative Services which provided the art work. Acknowledgements of individual contributions are made throughout the text and at the end.

In the first chapter 'Prelude to War' I have attempted to set the scene before that fateful September weekend. The second chapter covers the war years as remembered by the Villagers excluding Air Raids, Evacuees and Schooling which each have their own chapters. Another chapter is devoted to the many people who came into the area during the war "The Strangers" from Army, Navy, Air Force, Land Army; Americans, Germans and Italians while the last chapter deals with Victory.

CHAPTER 1

PRELUDE TO WAR

Robin Haworth moved to Nailsea from Darwen in Lancashire in 1932 leaving a cotton industry in decline to start a new life in Somerset. He and his family bought the 'Indian Bungalow' on Bucklands Batch and some land beside Cleeve Church to the west of Backwell where he now lives.

In 1937 or 1938 he attended a meeting where volunteers were asked for to help organise Civil Defence for the area. Air Raid Precautions (ARP) was probably the description used at the time with Civil Defence (referred to later as CD) covering a wider range of preparedness introduced about 1939.

He volunteered to help and became Chief Warden for an area covering Nailsea, Wraxall and Failand. Realising that this was much too large an area to cover on his own he went out to seek help.

At Nailsea West End he called on a gentleman by the name of Whitefield who lived near Court's Farm who agreed to be the contact for that area.

On his way back he called at Cherry Tree Farm where Jack Coombes undertook to look after Youngwood Lane.

At that time Mr R N Coate was living at the Battleaxes but agreed to look after Wraxall; by the time the War started he was living at St Johns Cottage in Wraxall.

Failand presented more of a problem but Robin was able to get help from a family called Hughes who lived on 'sixty acres' and Colonel Brittan (head of the shoe firm) who lived in Failand Hill House and agreed to look after the area surrounding the house.

In Nailsea at the Parish meeting of 1938, in answer to Mr Summerell's question, the Chairman said that the village was waiting a lead from Long Ashton District Council with regard to Air Raid precautions. A year later Robin Haworth told parishioners that following a census of the village

> *"The authorities know the requirements for gas masks and, if and when they are needed, they can be collected from the Institute at Nailsea by one person from each house. Until that time the gas masks will stay in Clevedon where the headquarters of the Civil Defence are."*

The government meanwhile, had made plans to evacuate children and mothers from big cities where their presence would do nothing to help the war effort. Since the mid 1920's it had been feared that there could be no protection against the bomber. In general terms the country was divided into danger, neutral and safe areas. Evacuation was recommended from danger to safe areas (of which the Villages were one) and plans were made locally to receive and billet evacuees if they arrived. While not of direct importance to this story the attacks on 'neutral' Bristol and its subsequent reclassification as a 'danger area' presented problems for those dealing with evacuation from the city in that nearly all nearby 'safe areas' were full of evacuees from elsewhere.

As this story unfolds you may wonder whether the 'safe area' designation for the Villages was indeed an accurate one.

In Nailsea the ARP had been looking for a stone built house with accommodation for the air raid wardens and which could speedily be strengthened when the time came. Gerald Stacey was approached in 1938 and agreed that his house in Silver Street could be used. He signed up with the ARP in February 1939 as Chief Warden for Nailsea and is remembered by many cycling up the road blowing his whistle to indicate that raiders were approaching or that the danger had passed.

Wardens Mr Whittard, Sid Carey, Duggie Marsh, Len Brake and John Gower are also remembered by many often riding bicycles and blowing whistles.

In one particular instance the presence of a warden in Bucklands Batch giving a warning enabled school teacher Janet Barton to get her pupils indoors to shelter shortly before a bomb, exploding near what is now the Perrings, caused damage to the building and would probably have caused injury to the children had they been outside.

The Women's Voluntary Services for Civil Defence (W.V.S) was formed about 1938 and under its chairman, Lady Reading, played a major part on the 'Home Front' and many of the Villagers joined. Mary Shepstone remembers making camouflage netting as part of her duties.

Other organisations that were less welcome were the Blackshirts who tried to recruit locally. Rumour has it that their headquarters were in Clevedon or Tickenham and someone in that area was detained under the "18B Regulations".

The IRA were engaged in a bombing campaign on the mainland. Villagers reading their papers on 26th August 1939 found reports of an explosion in Coventry killing 5 and injuring more than a dozen.

Diplomatic activity was increasing as the nations drifted inevitably towards war.

CHAPTER 2

THE HOME FRONT

In London on 31st August 1939 the decision was made to commence evacuation and the movement of children, mothers and expectant mothers began the next day.

Many arrived at Nailsea Station and walked to the halls at Backwell crossroads or were brought to Nailsea and allocated to different families in the area. Others were taken to Belmont House and moved on from there. Mr Sowerby and Mr Parker seem to have been in the front line in Backwell while Mr Michaelis arranged the distribution in Tickenham. (I am sure that many of the local women were vitally involved but unfortunately their names have not been forthcoming).

Other evacuees were taken to Weston-Super-Mare and were brought back to the Villages by coach. Whichever way they came they were accommodated by the dawn of Sunday 3rd September.

THE DAY WAR BROKE OUT

Clifford Kortright remembers

"The Rector of Chelvey Church had made arrangements that his daughter would stay at home and listen to the wireless and then come to church and hand him a note saying whether or not we were at war. She did so after the second lesson and he announced "We are at War"."

Eileen Derry was making the beds of the Misses Macmillan at Heath Cottage behind the Friendship Inn and heard through the open window the customers saying that we were at war with Germany.

Angela Whittard remembers her father being told when he drove into a garage to get petrol

"War has been declared"

"We drove home quickly to Oldfield House in West Town Backwell to get the blackout up".

Phyllis Stacey was on holiday at Paignton; on her return she found

"The house had been reinforced, sandbags were there and we had three evacuees who were moved shortly after to another billet as with the ARP work we could not manage them."

She also remembers

"The Chief Warden's duties in 1939 were not full time. When the 'Red Alert' came through (meaning 'enemy action is imminent') Mother and I would phone the various numbers we had been given. Among them was Mr Coate who looked after Wraxall and someone in Tickenham to alert that village."

THE ARP

Gerald Stacey had a business to run from his house Highdale in Silver Street and was able to fit this in with 'part time' duties. When however the decision was made that the job had to be full time he stood down allowing Les Stokes to take over with Jim White and Mr Cooksley. Not wishing to fail to do his bit Gerald moved to the Auxiliary Fire Service. Les was in the first-aid party for some time and in that capacity went to help in Bristol on some of the raids. Later he went on a course to learn Rescue work and towards the end of the war he was sent with colleagues to help in London during the 'doodle-bug attacks'.

Civil Defence course nr Malmesbury. (L – R) 1 Cooksley, 4 Les Stokes, 5 Albert Crumpler *(TS)*

While there he was ill and had to remain in his billet and remembers hearing a flying bomb's engine cut out and the long silence before there was a nearby explosion. Two CD workers from the area were killed while working at Westcliff on Sea.

BLACKOUT

In most places it was very effective and John Brain whose family were the village bakers in Backwell mentioned that it was not much fun driving with headlamp cowls that were fitted to all vehicles.

One of the results of the blackout was that buildings which could not easily be blacked out could not be used outside of daylight hours. Some church services had to take place in the afternoons.

Shops that stayed open after dark had to have an effective blackout and, of course, where a door opened into the street there had to be a light trap.

Shop windows were notoriously difficult to deal with efficiently and often had in addition to a blind, a black painted band round the outside edges. Windows were also treated in various ways to reduce the risk of injuries should flying debris or blast break the glass.

In Nailsea High Street the Co-Op were using black paint around the window edges enthusiastically applied by Don Baker and other members of the staff.

He recalled an event which followed

"We lads used to go over to Backwell some evenings and one night we saw light streaming from the window of a bungalow. We knocked at the door and told the lady of the house who, far from being pleased, tore us off a strip. Next day we remembered the black paint."

"We went again to Backwell; this time carrying the paint tin and a brush. The light still shone forth from the bungalow window and we crept into the garden intending to help the war effort. However someone opened the door so we scooted and went back to the crossroads. From there we went up Dark Lane. Everywhere we saw a streak of light we blacked it out."

"Eventually we returned towards Nailsea and saw the light still flowing from the window. Again we went into the garden and being undisturbed completely covered the window in paint. I am told she didn't wake up until the baker knocked on the front door quite late in the morning."

"As we left the garden the 'gentleman' with the paint brush fell over the flower garden and hit Ginger full in the middle of his raincoat with the paint brush."

"Next day one of the girls in the Co-Op said 'How did you get paint all over your coat?' and the secret was out."

"We were bound over for 12 months, the judge decided to treat it as a youthful escapade. We had to pay £1 towards putting it right."

CAMPAIGNS

During the war the Government inspired many campaigns. Probably the ones most remembered were National Savings and Dig for Victory but there were of course Salvage where we were encouraged to save paper and aluminium and street railings and gates were taken away.

The National Savings Organisation began in the First World War and had continued in being. In November 1939 the slogan "Lend to Defend the Right to be Free" was launched and during the war most schools, shops and offices had their own Savings Group or were associated with one. The "Squander-Bug" was invented as a cartoon figure to discourage the spendthrift.

Specific savings weeks were designated to provide equipment for the forces. In Nailsea the three campaigns "Salute the

Soldier" "Warship Week" and "Wings for Victory" are remembered and for some considerable time the certificates the parish received hung in the Parish Room at Old Church.

As far as I have been able to ascertain over £20,000 was raised in the village for each campaign and no doubt the inhabitants of the other three villages were equally generous. As an indication of the value of this amount I believe one Spitfire cost £5,000 while a bomber cost between £15 to £20 thousand pounds. In Warship Week the £27,000+ that was raised was slightly more than 1/5th the cost of a corvette.

Tom Greenwood in his book "60 years of Scouting in Nailsea" said that the scouts became expert collectors of salvage. In the first year of the war they collected 15 tons of paper. Douglas Marsh, Harry Summers and Alan Reed did much of the organising assisted by Mr Haworth and his tractor with Messrs Tuckey and Appleby and other volunteer car owners.

Later the troop trek cart and a horse with a four wheel truck loaned by Mr Alvis of East End Farm was used.

In Backwell, Stella Crafer was a member of a Girl Guide company run by the Misses Lambert and French. For their war effort the company collected waste paper and rags, picked blackberries for preserves and, on one occasion large quantitites of stinging nettles for drugs. These nettles were laid on the floor of Miss Lambert's school to dry and for weeks afterwards the premises were invaded by spiders.

Backwell Guides collecting salvage (SH)

Many people who spoke to me remembered the collection of aluminium. In recent years it has been fashionable to decry the value of this form of salvage forgetting, I believe, the sense of involvement with the war effort it brought to those who participated.

The removal of railings and gates caused some ill feeling in Nailsea not so much at what was taken but rather what was left. As late as 1944 a representative of the Ministry of Works Directorate of Emergency Works and Recovery visited Nailsea to examine certain items that had been left. After the visit some were removed and 'honour was satisfied'.

DIG FOR VICTORY

As with many campaigns enthusiasm did not always lead to the hoped for results. Far too often farmers were forced to plough land that was totally unsuitable. Many locals made the effort though and the Thatchers at Little Egypt dug up their lawns. Children were given time off school to help with the harvest and potato picking. Ray Llewellyn remembers working for Farmer Gregory (where Westway now is) and also for Ern Prideaux at Elm Farm.

In Nailsea a village produce association was formed through the initiative of Mr Stamp a retired school master who lived at Glenarrow and his neighbour William 'Bill' Atchley who was a Bristol solicitor.

The Nailsea and District Village Produce Association was the forerunner of the Horticultural Society. Bill was treasurer for over 20 years while Laurie Miles who took over from Mr Stamp as Secretary held the post for longer.

When Norman Baker joined he could buy one hundred weight (roughly 50 kg) of growmore for 21/- (£1.05).

"Fertilizer we bought in bulk and sold it in smaller quantities at a price that enabled us to buy the next lot but not to make a profit."

"There was a government subsidy on lime and this enabled it to be sold very cheaply."

THE FIRE SERVICE

It was only two years before the war started that Nailsea's grand new Fire Station was opened on Kings Hill. Before that the fire engine had been kept in various places including the shed behind the Royal Oak now used by one of the local amateur dramatic groups for storage of scenery.

There was a full time crew on duty at Clist & Rattles garage at Cambridge Batch and one of these was killed during an exercise early in the war. At Nailsea, Harry Wyatt was in charge for a number of years and led his men into Bristol and Weston. Harry had an auxiliary pump attached to his car and on at least two occasions Phyllis Stacey drove the old Austin with pump attached to Bristol and Weston to help fight the fires caused by German bombers.

Nailsea Fire Brigade (L – R) Lee Cannard, Albert Reed, Don Baker, Ivor Nicholas, Sam James, Herbert Gamlen, Gerald Stacey, Edgar Hurford, Unknown, Ted Thomas, Harry Wyatt, Frith *(PS)*

Petrol was short during the war but several people remember the pump (at the garage opposite where the Willows now emerges onto 'High Street'), marked to indicate that only certain vehicles such as the fire service could use it.

Norman Baker recalls

> *"Every time the warning went we had to go to the fire station; messengers, retained men plus AFS."*

The warning to which he refers was a siren mounted at the Fire Station. Nailsea never had an 'Air Raid Siren' despite several campaigns being fought to try to get one.

The photograph which appears above shows members of the Nailsea fire service. The precise date is not known but many of the individuals named in it were mentioned by those sharing their memories.

One disaster was averted only with luck. The engine of the vehicle had to be kept warm and was started at intervals. Those on duty slept in the leanto attached to the main building and due to some unfortunate circumstances the fumes were sucked into the sleeping quarters.

> *"One night we nearly all got gassed and had to evacuate the building. Dr Gornall closed it down for a time."*

Grace Champion remembers the fire watchers

> *"Duties were carried out by those who were old enough. One enthusiastic watcher was soundly rebuked by the head warden for coming on duty with a saucepan on her head instead of a tin helmet."*

THE HOME GUARD

First formed in May 1940 as the Local Defence Volunteers its name was changed very quickly to the Home Guard. (At about the same time the Observer Corps came into being but although enquiries have been made no information about this important force has been forthcoming and regrettably it cannot form part of this book).

Many people supplied information about the Home Guard and I have to thank Joyce Coyle for the cover photograph showing Mr Cudmore in what little uniform had been provided.

The Home Guard were short of rifles at the beginning but were eventually issued with American Springfield rifles of marginally smaller calibre as compared with the standard British Lee Enfield rifle (·300"/·303"). This difference was to present problems throughout the war as rifle ammunition for the two armies was not interchangeable.

To establish the force locally someone had to be placed in command and various names were considered with the task eventually being given to Admiral Sir Hugh Tweedie who was then living at Wraxall House. Lady Tweedie organised the Red Cross locally and the house was used as a clearing house for casualties.

Among the local officers of the 7th Somerset (Long Ashton) Battalion were Captain Chick (son in law of Commander Evans of Nailsea Court) and Captain Tuckey.

Home Guard *(VR)*

With the many long nights following days at work interspersed with air raids it is inevitable in the absence of invasion and action that it is the humorous anecdotes that have survived the intervening years. The participants own words tell these stories but the reader must remember that at the time these men and women were prepared with the minimum of weapons, to take on a German army that had swept across Europe and to fight even to the death. Many of them had fought in the 1914/18 war and now found themselves facing the same opponent.

It was exciting; frightening and at times funny.

Clifford Kortright said

"We were at the top of Brockley Combe in a thunderstorm when I became the only person I know to completely destroy a field wireless set. You weren't supposed to use these in a thunderstorm but I did and great flames came out of it."

Another story which as I heard it from two sources seems to be reliable was that one of the HG accidentally shot Captain Chick in the arm. This incident I believe took place during training at the Brotherhood Hall now Toc H.

With the HG there was an enormous age range as those who have followed the TV series Dad's Army will realise. Youngsters used to join before they were conscripted. Others were too old to join the Armed Forces and between these two extremes there were those who were on special jobs who were not called up to serve with the regular forces.

Marching became a problem as the speed of the young could not be matched by the old. Often the troops were split into groups of roughly equal abilities and at least one member rode a bike to keep up. Is this story apocryphal I wonder?

If the later comments in this chapter are biased towards Nailsea it is not because those in the HG from Tickenham, Wraxall and Backwell did less, it is merely that the information came more from those who were connected with Nailsea.

The Scouts acted as orderlies and cooks and gave demonstrations to the HG in bridge building.

John Brain remembered the Backwell company while Eric McEwen Smith told me that his father was in the Tickenham company, he believes Mr Simmons of Tickenham Court was the officer.

Mary Shepstone who lives on the Batch remembers the Home Guard taking up a position in her front garden which would give the troops a good view of movements from the station.

Len Elverd told me of a trench that was dug near the end of the footpath across Morgans Hill and many people have mentioned that the 'post' they had at the eastern end of the open ground on Morgans Hill was subsequently covered over but vestiges remain.

Clifford Kortright has a fund of memories of the HG and the following are but a few

"We used to go on guard at the Skittle Alley of the Ring of Bells. Six men and a corporal every night. They would call the others out if anything serious happened. Each person's turn came round every six or eight days."

"I happened to be on duty on the night of Christmas Day (probably 1943). As I didn't mind doing the night shift I arranged with the others I would go home to have dinner and would then come back but would then have to be relieved in time for me to do the morning milking."

"I enjoyed my dinner and enjoyed some cider with it. I returned to the Ring of Bells and found in the Skittle Alley a table with 6 pints of beer on it. The others said that the regulars had been treating them and they had always asked for one for me and 'there they are'."

"It was a long night and whenever I felt like it I had a drink. By morning I had a job to get anywhere or do anything but there seemed to be a lot more cows than usual. Things got a bit complicated."

"Eventually we moved from the pub because someone thought the enemy might try to blow the bridge at the station. There was a little tennis pavilion where Backwell Motors is now. The guard was divided into four two hour periods. With six men and one corporal one pair had to do two shifts. Sometimes as an alternative we each did a 20 minute shift before midnight."

"While we were down there at the hut, for want of anything better to do, they started to bet on whether the next train would be up or down, freight or passenger. I did very well out of that as I understood the telegraph bell signals at the nearby signal box. When the others found out they stopped playing that game."

Another person told me of an incident one night while the HG were on Morgans Hill. It led to the troops diving flat and Bob Hobbs appeared to have been seriously injured. He had felt a blow to his chest as he dived for cover and his uniform appeared to be wet with blood. He was carried from the dark of Morgans Hill probably to the Ring of Bells where they intended to summon medical help.

In the light it was discovered that he had struck his chest on a stone as he hit the ground but unfortunately a cow had passed that way earlier in the day. The dampness on his uniform did not look nor smell like blood!

VILLAGE LIFE

With many of the men of the village away in the armed forces and others doing voluntary service as well as their own jobs, life changed. It is questionable whether the blackout had a greater effect on villages than it did on towns. Those who lived in villages were more used to the darkness and neither group of people welcomed a 'bombers moon'. Under such a moon Vera Waite remembers the shadow of a German Bomber flitting across Farleigh. This may have been the time that bombs were dropped near Jubilee Inn, Flax Bourton.

Vera also remembers taking the children onto Backwell Hill where, in addition to an A.A. Battery, there was a training ground for troops.

Many of the villagers used to watch as the soldiers charged hanging sacks and bayonetted them with much enthusiasm and shouting. The troops could also be seen crawling around the countryside with blackened faces and on some of the exercises even came into the village. While training they lived in huts, most of which have vanished without trace.

The site had no running water and an army water tanker would call at Sully's garage on the main road to replenish supplies.

The soldiers made friends with the local people and Vera mentioned that sometimes a large piece of cheese was left on her wall to help out the meagre rations. Sometimes sweets were left for the children to find.

Near to the training site was a pond used by tanks apparently to check water proofing. They came on their own tracks from the direction of the Bridgwater Road ran down a ramp into the water, trundled through it and emerged, dripping, on the other side. Eventually after adjustments they would depart in the direction from which they came.

During the daylight there were few opportunities for social life and entertainment, and what few there were, were enjoyed with an enthusiasm that was built upon the dearth of such events.

Eating out was difficult. Jenny Wakeham remembers having lunch, with her mother and sister, once a week at the British Restaurant run by Mrs Cowlin and her team of helpers at the Brotherhood Hall. Among the helpers she mentions Mrs Pinegar, Mrs Greehill, Mrs Lewis, Mrs Thatcher and Mrs Howarth.

She also took part in concerts held at the Village Institute (Church House, Silver St.). These were produced by Barbara Macrae.

The landlords of the local pubs tried to look after their regulars. Freddie Williams of the Queens Head sent his son to find out why one of his regulars had not turned up; he was found to be dead in his shack in Moorfields Lane.

At the other end of the village in the Butchers Arms

"Mr and Mrs Keel gave the room at the top of the stairs for a dance every week. The money that was taken went to provide comforts for the forces."

"When any man from Nailsea came home on leave his first pint in that pub was free."

While most sport ceased with the outbreak of war the local lads started to play football again when the boys club formed by Mr A W E Stamp and Mr O Appleby fielded a team to play friendlies probably in 1942. Later the club became a member of the Affiliation of Boys Clubs League. The players used bike, bus or train to get to matches in Yatton, Clevedon, Portishead and Bristol.

The Americans took on local sides at Baseball and Cricket and at various local fetes events such as 'tug of war' took place. The Sheep Fair was held at the George Inn at Farleigh as it has been for many years. Angela cycled there probably with her sister Maureen and their evacuees Daphne and Audrey Wanford.

The local churches held services almost as usual but mostly during daylight hours. Angela mentions that the Catholic Church

"Was held in different places - the Royal Oak, the Scout Hut on Sunnymede, a garage at Trendlewood and then the hut at Ash Hayes Road."

The son of the Rector at Backwell achieved an honourable mention in the Evening Post as recorded by Isobel Robinson in her "Backwell Local Notes".

"March 23rd 1940 - The young soldier who, as reported in the Evening Post on Monday pluckily dived into the Harbour at the Centre and rescued a child who had fallen in the water and went away without giving his name, was Gunner O J Urch of the Royal Artillery whose home address is 'The Rectory', Backwell."

She also mentions in May that the local milestones and direction posts have been removed.

The large number of young men in the armed forces who came into the area were an inevitable attraction and one young girl found that her elder sister used her as an excuse to go for walks near the searchlight camps at West End and Cadbury. No doubt similar excursions were made to Backwell Hill.

In Nailsea, both the Institute and the Drill Hall were used for Dances, with the former being used as a cinema as well, as one contributor recalled remembering sitting in the back row with her boyfriend.

Dances were also held later in the war at the American hospital at Tyntesfield. The Americans would come to the village in a truck and take the girls back there for a dance and supper. Afterwards the girls were brought back to the village in the truck. No Americans were allowed to leave camp after the dance and the truck was often searched at the gate but this did not deter the more daring ones from hiding below the seats and chancing their luck on getting back later.

CHAPTER 3

VILLAGES UNDER ATTACK

Not unexpectedly most of those who have contributed to this book had memories of the air raids. How the Villages were ever regarded as a safe area is a mystery.

Little had happened in the area apart from the influx of evacuees dealt with elsewhere when on the day that the evacuation from Dunkirk began Isobel Robinson recorded that

> *"Local Defence Volunteers have been raised throughout the country to combat aeroplanes and crews and parachutists who may try to invade ..... the age limit (of the LDV) is 64."*

The first bomb found in the area was on the railway at Flax Bourton, it weighed about 4 lbs and was destroyed the following day (19th June 1940) by the military.

There were so many raids in the area that I have had to be selective and reduce in length many of the fascinating stories. The records at Taunton RO were particularly useful in helping to tie in stories with actual dates. Some of the entries in those records have been put in the Appendix for those who wish to know more.

The following is a more or less chronological story told mostly in the villagers own words or based closely on their accounts. With events taking place at night I have adopted the convention of denoting a particular night viz 1/2 July and have used the '24 hour clock' where that was employed in official reports. Complications have sometimes arisen in determining whether a date accompanying a particular report was the day it happened or the day the report was written. I regret any problems caused if the diary of events below is not as accurate as I would like.

July 1940 was a busy month for air raids but things were to get worse.

1/2 July	near Station Road, Nailsea 3 bombs
4 July	near Valley Farm, Tickenham 1 UXB (unexploded bomb)
15 July	Flares seen from Nailsea
	01.03 Believed UXB fell near military camp at Nailsea
	04.25 3 craters boundary Brockley/Cleeve near the church
19 July	Christchurch School Log records an air raid warning just as school was about to end so they stayed in the building until 5.20 pm

On the night of 1/2 August people found that a German raider had dropped leaflets "roughly the size of the Bristol Evening News." The report to Clevedon CD HQ stated that the subject of the leaflet was Hitler's speech to the Reichstag on 19.7.1940 and the leaflet did not contain any appeal. Most leaflets were gathered in by the authorities but a few escaped the net as the one reproduced here bears witness.

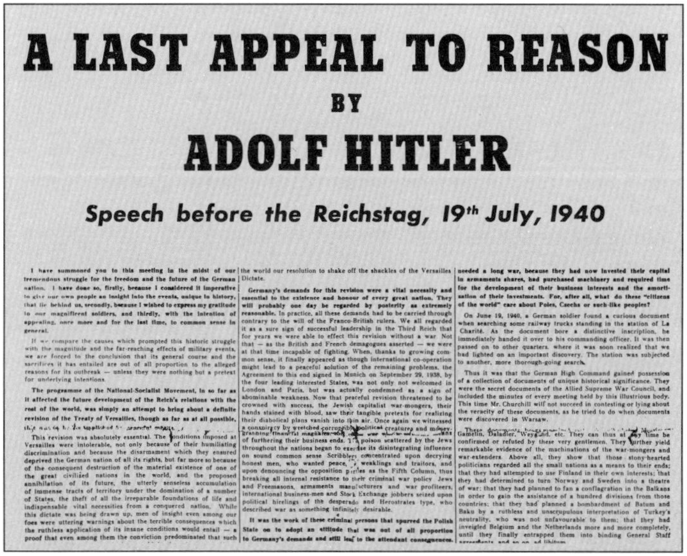

A LAST APPEAL TO REASON

BY

ADOLF HITLER

Speech before the Reichstag, 19th July, 1940

I have summoned you to this meeting in the midst of our tremendous struggle for the freedom and the future of the German nation. I have done so, firstly, because I considered it imperative to give our own people an insight into the events, unique in history, that lie behind us, secondly, because I wished to express my gratitude to our magnificent soldiers, and thirdly, with the intention of appealing, once more and for the last time, to common sense in general.

If we compare the causes which prompted this historic struggle with the magnitude and the far-reaching effects of military events, we are forced to the conclusion that its general course and the sacrifices it has entailed are out of all proportion to the alleged reasons for its outbreak — unless they were nothing but a pretext for underlying intentions.

The programme of the National-Socialist Movement, in so far as it affected the future development of the Reich's relations with the rest of the world, was simply an attempt to bring about a definite revision of the Treaty of Versailles, though as far as at all possible, [illegible]

This revision was absolutely essential. The conditions imposed at Versailles were intolerable, not only because of their humiliating discrimination and because the disarmament which they ensured deprived the German nation of all its rights, but far more so because of the consequent destruction of the material existence of one of the great civilized nations in the world, and the proposed annihilation of its future, the utterly senseless accumulation of immense tracts of territory under the domination of a number of States, the theft of all the irreparable foundations of life and indispensable vital necessities from a conquered nation. While this dictate was being drawn up, men of insight even among our foes were uttering warnings about the terrible consequences which the ruthless application of its insane conditions would entail — a proof that even among them the conviction predominated that such [illegible] the world our resolution to shake off the shackles of the Versailles Dictate.

Germany's demands for this revision were a vital necessity and essential to the existence and honour of every great nation. They will probably one day be regarded by posterity as extremely reasonable. In practice, all these demands had to be carried through contrary to the will of the Franco-British rulers. We all regarded it as a sure sign of successful leadership in the Third Reich that for years we were able to effect this revision without a war. Not that — as the British and French demagogues asserted — we were at that time incapable of fighting. When, thanks to growing common sense, it finally appeared as though international co-operation might lead to a peaceful solution of the remaining problems, the Agreement to this end signed in Munich on September 29, 1938, by the four leading interested States, was not only not welcomed in London and Paris, but was actually condemned as a sign of abominable weakness. Now that peaceful revision threatened to be crowned with success, the Jewish capitalist war-mongers, their hands stained with blood, saw their tangible pretexts for realizing their diabolical plans vanish into thin air. Once again we witnessed a conspiracy by wretched corruptible political creatures and money-grabbing financial magnates [illegible] means of furthering their business ends. The poison scattered by the Jews throughout the nations began to exercise its disintegrating influence on sound common sense. Scribblers concentrated upon decrying honest men, who wanted peace, as weaklings and traitors, and upon denouncing the opposition parties as the Fifth Column, thus breaking all internal resistance to their criminal war policy. Jews and Freemasons, armaments manufacturers and war profiteers, international business-men and Stock Exchange jobbers seized upon political hirelings of the desperado and Herostrates type, who described war as something infinitely desirable.

It was the work of these criminal persons that spurred the Polish State on to adopt an attitude that was out of all proportion to Germany's demands and still led to the attendant consequences. [illegible] needed a long war, because they had now invested their capital in armaments shares, had purchased machinery and required time for the development of their business interests and the amortisation of their investments. For, after all, what do these "citizens of the world" care about Poles, Czechs or such-like peoples?

On June 19, 1940, a German soldier found a curious document when searching some railway trucks standing in the station of La Charité. As the document bore a distinctive inscription, he immediately handed it over to his commanding officer. It was then passed on to other quarters, where it was soon realized that we had lighted on an important discovery. The station was subjected to another, more thorough-going search.

Thus it was that the German High Command gained possession of a collection of documents of unique historical significance. They were the secret documents of the Allied Supreme War Council, and included the minutes of every meeting held by this illustrious body. This time Mr. Churchill will not succeed in contesting or lying about the veracity of these documents, as he tried to do when documents were discovered in Warsaw.

These documents [illegible] Gamelin, Daladier, Weygand, etc. They can thus at any time be confirmed or refuted by these very gentlemen. They further yield remarkable evidence of the machinations of the war-mongers and war-extenders. Above all, they show that those stony-hearted politicians regarded all the small nations as a means to their ends; that they had attempted to use Finland in their own interests; that they had determined to turn Norway and Sweden into a theatre of war; that they had planned to fan a conflagration in the Balkans in order to gain the assistance of a hundred divisions from those countries; that they had planned a bombardment of Batum and Baku by a ruthless and unscrupulous interpretation of Turkey's neutrality, who was not unfavourable to them; that they had inveigled Belgium and the Netherlands more and more completely, until they finally entrapped them into binding General Staff agreements and so on ad libitum.

The CD records report 2 bombs being dropped on 9th August at 5.50 am. One of these fell at Tickenham. A particular point made about this is that the bombs fell shortly after the message "white" was received. By way of explanation the method of warning local CD units of impending enemy activity was by transmitting a word representing a colour. This enabled the recipient to judge the actual state of affairs and allowed factories to continue to work as long as it was safe to do so.

The code used was Yellow, Purple, Red, White. Yellow and Purple were preliminary stages of 'preparedness' while Red meant enemy action imminent, white meant part time CD personnel could be dismissed. This usually came after enemy aircraft had been gone for some time hence the concern when bombs fell out of an 'empty sky'.

The CD report said that the Area Officer had just returned, he had investigated the site at Tickenham and found that

> *"HE (High explosive) bombs had exploded in Tower House Wood near the bottom of Tickenham Hill causing damage to roofs ceilings and windows and doors of six houses. Slight damage to others. No casualties."*

This is almost certainly the raid described by Eric McEwen-

Smith. He said that while many people thought this was a land mine he felt it more likely to have been a sea mine that went a bit off target.

To some extent this view seems very likely as the CD had been warned on 10th July about magnetic mines

"(These) are two feet in diameter, 9 feet long with 1500 lbs of High Explosive dropped with a parachute 27 feet in diameter. It falls at 40 mph. It has a special fuse to cause it to explode if it falls on land. In water it acts as a magnetic mine. If seen contact the Naval Authorities."

Eric was living with his parents at Hales Farm and was in bed when the explosion happened. His father said to him after the bang.

"I think a ruddy bomb has dropped somewhere."

"We put on some clothes and went downstairs hell for leather and fell over the front door which had been blown in and up the stairs. Then we went through a passageway where mother kept a lot of crockery and patent medicines for the cattle. There was broken glass everywhere and we had no shoes on."

"Out in the yard we found pretty well all the buildings had been stripped of tiles. The cattle were all right."

"We went out into the road and someone said it had fallen in the woods. Next day we found out where. Trees had vanished for about 30 yards around and others had been shredded like matchsticks."

The CD report on this incident went on to say

"One unusual feature of the bomb was the heat of it which was felt 3/4 mile away. This is confirmed by the Police Constable and Wardens. Traces in the wood were smouldering one hour after the explosion. A piece of metal picked up on the site appeared to be fused aluminium alloy."

At 09.17 on Monday 12th August there was a report of a whistling bomb falling between Elm Farm and a house called the Elms. On 20th August there was a report of a bomb in Back Lane. Neither had exploded and nothing was found on either occasion. Two HE fell behind Folly Farm about 22.45 on 30th August.

Isobel Robinson recorded on 11th September that two bombs dropped near the Railway Station and it was rumoured a third went down a mine shaft. I can find nothing else recorded for that day and wonder whether this is a reference to the incident referred to above on 1/2 July. There are other entries in her notes that lead me to believe the date is merely the date of the entry and not the date of the incident.

On 16th September the CD HQ learned of a UXB near the searchlight at Cadbury Camp subsequently to be told by the police that it had fallen at New Farm. On the same day a further report brought to their attention one HE at Young Wood Farm N of the GWR line - crater 25 feet in diameter.

All that had gone before paled into insignificance to the events of 25th September 1940 and many are the stories I was told of this day that was etched in everyone's memories who was in one of the villages that day.

Imagine if you can looking from Tickenham Hill on a fine summer's day with the sea and Steep Holm in the background and seeing a large formation of aircraft turning towards you.

Fifty years ago this was the sight Bill Yendole saw as he worked with Roy Coker in the latter's market garden. Even in these days it was unusual to see so many aircraft at once and he continued to look as they headed towards him. It didn't take long for him to realise what they were

"Look Roy, that's bloomin Jerries coming up over Weston."

It was the day of the Filton Raid!

Robin Haworth had heard from Redvers Coate earlier that morning when he phoned to say that as he was going to London on business would Robin look after Wraxall should there be a raid. Robin had said he would and had gone to work at his nursery beside Cleeve Church.

He too heard the roar of engines and saw the aircraft, realised they were German and saw them turn towards Bristol on a course that would take them along the railway line. He still feels that the Germans were using this to navigate by. There was one fighter attacking the formation.

"Because I had to cover Wraxall I got in the car, teeth chattering. I came up the Batch passing where I lived and saw that was intact and passed a bomb crater on the left before the house where the Methodist Parson lived."

"I went on to Wraxall saw the prisoner by the side of the top road with the Home Guard and went on down Portbury Lane where I saw the plane crashed on the right. It was on fire and a few bombs had rolled out; machine gun bullets were popping off."

The attack on Filton took place at 11.48 and it was therefore approximately 11.40 when the formation passed over Nailsea apparently without opposition as the fighter seen earlier had had to leave and other fighters did not make contact until moments before bombs were dropped at Filton. This gave more than one of the watchers the feeling that the Germans must already have taken over the southern part of England to be able to fly in formation as if on an exercise.

Monica Freeman ran up the road to a neighbour and found when she got there that she had a carving knife in one hand and a carrot in the other while Margaret Frogley did not believe her husband when he called to her to come to see the German aircraft.

Eric McEwen-Smith was horse hoeing with others at Hales Farm in Tickenham and thought the planes were British. He found he was wrong when the AA gun at Markham opened up.

"The horse tried to bolt but Charlie managed to hang on to him. We hitched everything off and ran for cover."

At another farm in Tickenham a land girl and a chap were hoeing swedes and carried on hoeing as the planes came over. When the explosions and gun fire started she said over her shoulder *"do you think we had better take cover?"* Getting no reply she turned round and saw him disappearing out of the field gate.

It was rumoured that all the AA guns had been dismantled for cleaning except the one at Markham and it was this one that fired and scored a hit. One or two eye witnesses claimed to have seen the odd British fighter engaging the very large force of over 50 bombers and about 40 fighters. It seems that these attacks and gunfire caused two or three aircraft to break from the formation and release bombs in the area while the hit by the AA gunfire brought the plane down at Failand.

Thelma Stokes was at a cookery class in the upstairs room at the Butchers Arms

"We heard a lot of planes and recognised the engines as German. We looked out of the window. They were virtually overhead - we could see them all. Our teacher said we must go down the cellar. We came down the outside steps of the Butchers Arms and found ourselves in a passage way lined each side with bottles."

Janet Barton at her school at St Leonards just got the children indoors before a bomb exploded nearby blowing in a window frame. Mrs Vance in Station Road was talking to a neighbour and had her little girl with her

"We looked up to see this wonderful display of planes coming over. When they were nearly overhead we realised they had black crosses on them and that they were Germans. I shall never forget the moment. I thought if they have got here the Germans must have conquered all the southern part of England."

In Backwell, Vera Waite's friend was worried as she watched the aerial armada head towards Bristol. Her husband was there working not far from the rugby ground

"We thought it was the invasion as we saw some bale out of the planes flying up the valley."

Also in Backwell, Stella and her friends watched in admiration. They thought at first the planes were Royal Air Force but soon found they were mistaken.

In Silver Street the children who had been having lessons at the Brotherhood hall had crossed the road to Moorfield House and were filing into the cellars. As the planes came overhead John Gowar the headmaster told them to hurry. He had looked up and realised the planes were German.

Clifford Kortright takes up the story from his viewpoint up a damson tree at Brockley Elm farm where he was working with another labourer

"We heard the planes flying overhead. We thought they were ours going out to meet something. There was a lot of banging and whistling and we decided there were machine gun bullets flying around. We came down the ladders in record time and went into the road that was between two high banks which we thought would provide protection."

"We stayed there for what seemed like 5 minutes. There was a devil of a roar going on and we could hear big explosions. We decided it was not very interesting where we were so we went and leaned on six acres gate which was at the top of the rise."

"We had a sort of ringside seat and after it all quietened down we went back to picking damsons.

"It was a lovely day with blue sky and great big lumps of white cloud. We could see planes going in and out of the cloud and I remember seeing one of the chaps parachuting down swinging like a pendulum. Something must have been wrong for it to go like that."

Several people noticed that one had trouble with his parachute. Maybe it was the one Robin saw at the roadside who was taken by ambulance to Clevedon where

"Some fool women took him flowers."

Unexploded Bomb! (RL)

Many bombs were dropped in the area. A copy of the CD report is in the Appendix. There were no casualties in the

Villages apart from the airman who suffered leg fractures. The only damage was the water main to Tyntesfield House which was cut and a farm house and out-building on the Tyntesfield Estate.

Norman Baker was watching from outside Hewetts shop with Francis Durbin and both were lucky not to have been injured when a large piece of shrapnel fell behind them. Some machine gun bullet cases were found later in the High Street.

Having successfully attacked Filton the German Heinkels and their Messerschmitt Bf 110 escort had to fight their way south as the RAF fighters engaged them.

Norman Searle was that day out in a van near Radstock and saw the engagement. Not far from where he stood watching he saw a Heinkel hit and some of the crew bale out. The German rear gunner continued to engage our fighters and hit one that crashed near the German plane. Both the gunner and the British pilot were killed.

That specific raid was over but there were many more to come. RAF Lulsgate Bottom started to be used for dual training before the month was out. Strangely enough the airfield was only a short distance from a 'decoy' set up to show lights to attract German bombers away from Bristol. While it was successful as will be recounted later it made life at night in Backwell West Town during raids rather frightening.

CD reports of two raids on 17/18 November are shown in the Appendix. The first raid caused two deaths at the New Inn at Lulsgate while in the second 16 bombs dropped between Tickenham and Nailsea. One of these fell within twenty yards of the Causeway but did not explode. The Causeway was closed until it had been dealt with.

The night of 24th November was the first very heavy raid on Bristol and although no bombs were dropped near the Villages many of the inhabitants remembered being able to read their newspaper outside in the light of the fires in Bristol.

In December, Isobel Robinson noted that people were flocking out of Bristol and in January 1941 she refers to the raids on Weston Super Mare.

1941

There was a heavy raid on Bristol which started on 3rd January and continued for 12 hours ending early on the next morning. The weather was so cold that water from the hoses being used to fight the fires froze where it fell.

In Wraxall that night a bomb fell about 70 yards north of the Rectory. The Bomb Disposal Squad (BDS) examined the crater on the following morning and were apparently satisfied. They kept the vanes. Cyril Wilcox remembers the crater being re-examined. In it was found a UXB of 1400 kilograms; sufficient, if it had exploded, to have destroyed the church. The bomb was removed on 15th July 1941.

There were other raids in January; on the night of 4/5 January many incendiaries were dropped in the area with some HE scattered around. (For details see Appendix).

It may have been the occasion when an incendiary dropped into the bulls house at Hales farm. Eric said

"The old bull in there was roaring his head off. There was a blue flame inside there. We didn't know what to do. One of the men said I'll let a cow out and turn her down the yard behind. Then I'll open the door and let him out that way."

"While he was doing that the bull pushed the flaming straw and a bomb into the yard at the front. His eyes were blazing and we thought we would have to shoot him."

"Then the cow was let out the back and we opened the door and the bull went quietly."

"The bomb had dropped through the roof but the bull had not been hurt. While he was out of the yard we were able to go in and stamp the flames out. On one occasion we picked up 78 bombs and fins in one field after a raid on Avonmouth."

Another raid took place on 16/17 January and left one person dead near Long Ashton Golf Club with a bomb and numerous incendiaries at Lower Failand while at 22.30 there was a report of an UXB falling in a field on Backwell Common Farm.

Twelve HE and some incendiaries fell on 3/4 March near the Jubilee Inn at Flax Bourton.

Sunday 16th March was the evening when another major attack took place on Bristol. Isobel Robinson recorded that the raid lasted from about 9.15 pm until 4.00 am. On the following day she had spoken to Mr Coles the owner of the quarry and he had told her of an unexploded bomb behind it; she records also meeting Mrs Cowlin - she was on her way to the Food Control Office for advice as the hall in Silver Street used for communal feeding had been badly damaged.

The Christchurch School Log on 17th March revealed

"We had a heavy raid last night and many houses in Nailsea were damaged so few children arrived and the registers were not marked."

That same night about 150 HEs dropped in Brockley Woods (attracted by the Decoy) together with many incendiaries. Despite this only one house was damaged but there were many UXB's.

In Nailsea eight HE bombs fell on Youngwood Farm while 4 HE fell between Netherton Wood and South Common Farm.

There was however a further bomb which landed in the middle of Nailsea and caused considerable damage and yet despite the number of people living nearby did not cause any physical injury to anyone. It landed in Moorfields Lane (now Fosse Lane) just off Silver Street.

Ray Llewellyn remembers

"Uncle Sam had a house in Moorfields Lane; the bomb blew doors and windows out and some tiles off the roof. The family were under the table and when the dust settled they found the handles of the cups still hanging on the dresser. All the cups had been broken."

"The fish and chip shop had its big window blown out. It was patched up with wood and felt etc in the centre of which was a small window about 12 inches square. It stayed like that for the rest of the war."

Len Stokes who lived (and still lives) across the road near to the fish shop told me

"We had our roof blown off and the blackout blown in. Every pane in the greenhouse opposite was broken."

Len was in the CD rescue party and was about to leave for Bristol when they heard a bomb had fallen in Silver Street. The party left not knowing where or whether there had been injuries to their families. Fortunately when he got to the Muller orphanage he found his nephew in charge of the CD. He was able to contact Nailsea and reassure the party that there had been no casualties.

Angela Whittard remembers the night they hit the decoy.

"We were under the table in the dining room that night; next day we went out picking up shrapnel. It was only later that we realised there could have been unexploded bombs in the area (In fact there were)."

The day after the raid Basil Greenhill asked the Chairman of Nailsea Parish Council if he would consider making application for the sounding of a siren for Air Raid Warnings in the Parish. The Chairman pointed out that previous requests had not been granted.

Having been on the edge of an area that was heavily bombed without suffering any damage Oldfield House and the Whittards were to find that it only needed one bomb in the right, or should I say wrong place to provide far more danger. On April 4th a bomb dropped very near to the house damaging the roof severely and bringing part of it down. Angela and Maureen were under the piano and safe despite extensive damage to other parts of the house.

"It was deadly quiet; it was also pitch black because the bomb had cut off the electricity supply."

"After a while we saw the flickering of torches and called out. The wardens called back to us to stay where we were because it was unsafe."

The old adage that lightning never strikes twice in the same place was soon brought into doubt. One week later another stick of bombs fell almost in the same places blowing the tarpaulin off the roof. Damage was done to Firgrove and the Gallops and a horse was killed. The Badminton House at West Town used by the school evacuated from Hammersmith, London was damaged and was out of use until 12th May.

On the night of 3/4 April 1UXB fell in a field 300 yards SE of the Battleaxes public house while the same night one Heinkel 111 was shot down by a Bristol Beaufighter; the German plane crashed at Hewish.

It was probably about this time that Robin Haworth met a lorry that had brought an UXB from Bristol to be blown up in the open fields. He and the driver decided the best place would be a crater in the fields and guided the lorry to the spot but was then horrified when he realised the driver intended to tip it in the hole. When he remonstrated he was told

"It's fallen a lot further than this already"

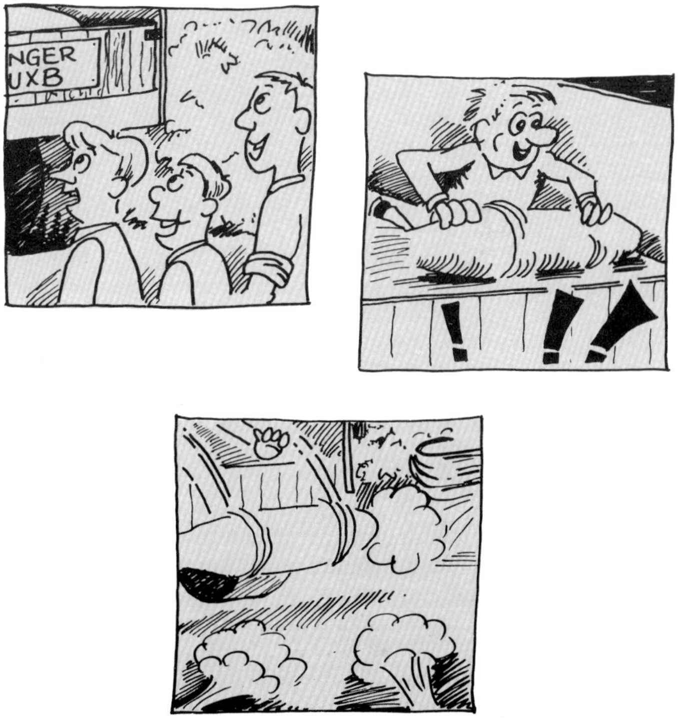

and it was pushed off the lorry into the hole. A detonating charge was got ready and the fuse lit and the charge dropped in onto the bomb. A very quick scamper to a safe distance was followed by a very loud explosion leaving a crater about the size of a two storey house.

Reports of 'UXB at Dibdens Farm' and 1 UX AA Shell in the field known as Long Ground of Grove Farm, Backwell were received on 15th April.

On 1/2 May 1941 four high explosive bombs were dropped in Tickenham near the junction of Failand and Nailsea crossroads. The Failand portion of the road was blocked for some time by a cattle trough with portions of a wall thrown into the road. Damage was reported mainly to roofs windows, doors and buildings of Old Well Farm (Mr Durston), the Elms (Dyer), The Gables (Birt), Stonedge Farm (Franks), The Star Inn (Nunn) and to properties of Messrs Charlton, Bye, Baker, Wilmot and Tucker. Mrs Baker's cottage next to Stonedge Cottages with Stony Batch cottages were also damaged. One bomb fell near the electric grid pylon.

At the end of the month another 'landmine' landed at 01.00 31 May in a field at the end of Heath Road (roughly where Greenfield Crescent now is) and exploded killing a cow belonging to the Misses MacMillan and leaving an immense crater. Much has already been written of this event but it seems worth letting those who were in Nailsea that night record their memories. Although the explosive force of the mine caused little damage the clay from the crater that was 26 feet deep and 60 feet across caused considerable minor damage when it came back to earth.

Some lumps were quite large and it is a wonder that nobody was killed and hardly any injured. I was told how Mrs Hobbs, who lived in a cottage (on the corner of what is now Link Road where Hobbs Court now stands), had a close escape from death. Bob was out on duty, her children were sleeping in one downstairs room and she was sleeping in another

> *"A lump of clay landed on the roof crashed through it and the upstairs floor and hit her bed knocking it through the floor."*

She was unharmed but very shaken while the children were untouched.

Other pieces of clay fell through roofs in other parts of the village one piece hitting the roof of Christ Church and causing damage which could be seen for years after.

On 5th June, Charlton Lodge and Tyntesfield received 18 small HE bombs at 02.30 in a line from the Lodge then down the private road from Upper Lodge to Tyntesfield Farm. Windows, ceilings and telephone lines were damaged; 3 cows were killed and 4 seriously wounded.

On 16/17 June 1941 death came to Nailsea. A German bomber was heard and then was seen struggling to escape from the searchlight beams as the AA opened up. It turned away from Bristol flying low towards the west. As it crossed between Wraxall and Nailsea its pilot must have decided to jettison his bomb load. 15 bombs fell in a line from 270 yards south of the Kennels to 200 yards north east of Coombe Grange. (See Appendix).

Nowhere before the bomb. The Derry family and Mrs Austin (ext right). *(EJ)*

At Nowhere there were three cottages, one detached where the Derry family lived, the other two semi-detached. In one of these lived the Austins and two lodgers, the other was not occupied but contained the furniture belonging to Mr Gilbert Thomas and his family who were to move in on 17th June.

Eileen Derry was under the stairs; she heard the plane coming and then the sound of bombs exploding and getting ever nearer until one was very close and then the noises receded.

One bomb had hit the two cottages roughly where the joining wall was. Len Summers emerged from the damaged cottage knowing the Austins had been injured. With Eileen he ran up the lane to get Dr Gornall. When they got to the main road they found a number of people had gathered uncertain as to what had happened. Eileen told them to go down to Nowhere to help as someone was injured; at that time she didn't know that Mr Austin had been killed and his wife seriously injured.

Another lodger, Len Pearce, made his way across the fields to Elm Farm and came across a field where a bomb had fallen into a herd of cows killing five and wounding three. What was bad at night must have seemed worse by daylight when the extent of the mutilation could be seen.

A second building on the west of Station Road was hit. It

was one of a pair of bungalows now not far from the junction with Queens Road.

The occupants of the bungalow (the Thorburn family) were in their Anderson shelter in the garden and were unhurt as were the two ladies who lived in the adjoining bungalow who, I am told, were unaware of their near miss until the next day.

Monica Freeman, the Austin's daughter, lived with her husband in a cottage on the 'Score', the road from Nailsea to Wraxall not very far from where the Esso garage now stands.

She and her husband Alf were just going to bed having heard the bombs fall when there was a knock at the door. She went to the window and could see Roy Harvey at the door. Opening the window she called to him to find out what he wanted. He replied

"Is your husband there? I want to speak to him."

"Alfie got dressed and went downstairs. After speaking to Roy he went off with him."

Monica went downstairs and waited outside knowing that something had happened at Nowhere. While she was waiting a car went past. It was Dr Gornall. He saw her, stopped and backed up. He asked her what she was doing and where was her husband? She told him that she thought Alfie had gone to Nowhere. He replied

"He shouldn't have gone - we don't know how many bombs have dropped."

Dr Gornall *(MS)*

Monica was told that her father George had been killed and that her mother had been seriously injured. She told me

"Mother was taken to Wraxall House and was then taken to Clevedon Cottage Hospital and finished up at Winford for about eighteen months. A piece of shrapnel had gone through her ankle. At one time a specialist wanted to amputate her foot."

Depite this Alice Austin made a recovery and although often in pain continued to do her own shopping until she was about 90. She died in 1967 aged 92.

Just over a month after the raid the workmen preparing RAF Lulsgate were surprised when a Junkers Ju 88 landed having mistaken its whereabouts.

The CD records do not record any more raids in 1941 and there is not much in 1942 that affected the Villages apart from sending personnel to Weston Super Mare during raids on that town (see Appendix).

On December 31st 1942 there is a note in the CD diary to the effect that there had been 541 'Red Alerts' to date. Of these only 61 took place in 1942. In the eighteen months from July 1940 to December 1941 there had been an average of 6 a week in the Clevedon CD area.

CHAPTER 4

EVACUATION

Plans to evacuate the children and mothers-to-be were first mooted in the mid 1920's when it was feared there would be no protection against the bomber. In the months before the outbreak of war, schools, in the danger areas, had several rehearsals in gathering together the children whose names were down to go. They would arrive at school carrying small cases or brown paper parcels 'tied up with string' containing a change of clothes.

As the months of 1939 passed by it became more and more obvious that we could soon be at war. The hopeful kept saying

'if we are not at war tomorrow there won't be a war!'

On the 31st of August a decision was made to commence the evacuation on the following day. Many people heard it from friends or from the schools while others heard too late that plans had been changed.

While the movement of children away from London was a gigantic undertaking little credit has been given to those who organised the transfer of trainloads of tired, hungry, wet and unhappy children from their arrival point to the reception area or areas and their allocation to volunteer 'foster parents'. Inevitably some of the homes provided were unloving, some loving, but most provided a welcome for youngsters of differing backgrounds. Some children had never been out of the big city. Some wanted to go home, some went home and some stayed and became one of the family.

This then is the background to the biggest population movement ever seen in the British Isles.

I have been able to talk to many people who knew evacuees or had them billeted on them or their parents. It has been surprisingly difficult to obtain information from people who were evacuated as children to Nailsea but great help has been forthcoming from Ivy Port who came to Nailsea by accident with three young children on the first weekend of the war. In Backwell I have been luckier in having been able to trace five young ladies who came with the North Hammersmith Central School. Joyce Coyle was 15 at the time, Daphne Wanford, Stella Crafer and Grace Champion 13 and Louise Cook who was nearly 12. I have visited Joyce and spoken with Daphne and Stella on the telephone and received a letter with details from Louise in Canada and from Grace in Australia. In addition the two daughters of the house where Daphne stayed, Angela and Maureen Whittard have provided photos and memories. This then is their chapter.

PREPARATIONS TO LEAVE LONDON

Ivy Port had arranged to go with the Essendine Road School in Kilburn but its plans were changed and it went a day early leaving her behind. She was able to make arrangements with another school for the next day. It was a terrific rush as she had to leave on the Sunday at 6 am with three young children. She remembers her husband whose birthday it was saying "Don't wish me a happy birthday today." At the Hammersmith School the pupils used to gather waiting for the word to go. Then they went home to do some washing which was then hung in front of the fire to dry to be ready for the next day. On the Friday they were told they would be away on Saturday 2nd September. It was a very tense time that brought a tear to many an eye. In London they had been digging up the parks and putting in air raid shelters and also bringing smaller shelters to houses.

It seems likely from the stories told about the evacuation that the girls of the Hammersmith School travelled in two groups one alighting from their train at Nailsea the other going on to Weston and being bussed to Backwell.

Louise Cook remembered

"The tube ran along the back of our garden. I can still see my mum and dad and the neighbours waving towels at the trains but I learnt later they did not see us but kept waving all day just in case we were on one."

Joyce Coyle said

"We went off to school that morning with our clothes that had been washed. Tempers had been on edge, we had no idea where we were going. We went in crocodile to Shepherds Bush underground station and then to one of the stations in Ealing where we changed trains."

Daphne has memories of waiting for buses in London and was excited to be going on a train. She had a bag of emergency rations for her sister aged 9 and her brother 15. She felt important to be given charge of the supplies which were to be taken from her very suddenly as will be explained in due course.

Louise had with her a younger brother and sister while Joyce travelled with her brother Maurice.

ARRIVAL

When the train arrived at Nailsea, Daphne with her brother and sister walked up to the crossroads where the Parish Hall and WI Hut stood. I believe Louise came the same way but Joyce with other children got off a train at Weston and were bussed back. Having been born in Bristol, and having relations there, Joyce was pleased to find the bus taking them in that direction. Stella also remembers arriving at Weston.

Ivy found the Red Cross waiting and was directed to a coach, it was about noon by then. Not knowing any of the people she had travelled with she didn't find out that she was on the wrong coach until she got to the Drill Hall.

"The driver (Jack Cutler) asked me if I'd like to go back to Weston to see where my party had gone but I'd had enough travelling with the kiddies and said I would stay."

"We all went into the hall and were given a carrier bag with sugar, butter, a tin of corned beef, a tin of milk and some biscuits."

To avoid causing confusion before we return to the children converging on Backwell crossroads let us follow Ivy Port's initial experiences in Nailsea.

After being taken by car to three different places, where a mother and three children were not welcomed, Ivy returned to the Hall. Here she and the children were allocated a room in a house in Nailsea Park (where the owner used to walk about with her cat in her arms singing hymns).

After a few months of this she saw a notice "cottage to rent 7/- (35p) a week." It was owned by Dr Reg White's mother, a tiny lady. Ivy went to the house in Silver Street opposite Back Lane (now Whitesfield Road) and spoke to her. She was told there were many local people after it and she didn't have much of a chance.

However after Ivy explained her position the old lady took pity on her and let her have it saying

"I am afraid you will have to put up with some bitterness from the local people – you know what local people are like. They won't like it a bit if I let it to an outsider."

Ivy sent up to London for some furniture and moved in. Maybe the locals relented a little as the first Christmas she was there

"I went out to the gate to get some water and there was a carrier bag on the gate 'from Father Christmas' with toys for the children. To this day I don't know who put it there."

In Nailsea, the children from Wornington Road School had settled in.

At weekends coaches would come bringing parents of some of the children. Inevitably this caused disappointment for some of the children who waited on the village green outside the shops.

It is worth pausing for a moment to remember the pressures that evacuation placed on many of the children who had to be 'mother/father' to their younger brothers and sisters.

We now return to Backwell during that fateful weekend in September 1939.

Daphne and her sister with their brother were chosen

Waiting for Mum and Dad (JS)

There's a coach coming in (JS)

"Hooray! Dad's on leave" (JS)

quickly by Mr Parker who it seemed was head of the 'selectors'. Because of this they had to wait until homes were found for the others.

For most of her 2½ years in Backwell, Stella was billeted with Mr and Mrs Shaw in Dark Lane.

Louise and Joyce had rather less pleasant experiences as they watched women walking around picking who they wanted. The longer Louise and her brother and sister waited the harder they cuddled together.

"Finally we and two other kids were taken to the 'Gentry's House'. Very scared we sat round the table with a maid coaxing us to eat. When she served my tea her fingers slipped from the teapot and the tea scalded my arm. Then there were tears from everyone."

In her book "Keep Smiling Through" – Susan Briggs mentions a confidential report by a headmaster of a school evacuated to the West Country who said that billeting officers will not billet children on their friends so the cottages have evacuees while the big houses do not. He went on to say that in these districts the feudal system was still in full swing and the cottagers dare not refuse to have children.

Whatever the reason Vera Waite who had arrived too late at the 'share out' of the evacuees was asked by Mr Sowerby from the big house whether she would have two sisters. Vera had two bedrooms and two children herself (a small girl and a baby boy) but was persuaded to take the two girls while their brother Ronnie went to Coles Farm just across the road. So Louise and Winnie Cook arrived and they all got on wonderfully. Winnie even taught the baby to walk.

When all the children had been sorted out, including Louise and Joyce who I will return to later, Mr Parker took Daphne and the other two children to his large house overlooking the railway line.

"After my sister and I went to bed I got up and took a bar of chocolate out of the emergency rations giving us half each."

"We had hardly started eating when Mr Parker came to see why we were still talking. He was furious with me and said I should have given the food to Mrs Parker."

"We stayed there about three weeks but when it became apparent that invasion was not imminent my sister and I were moved. My brother stayed until November when the exam he was to have taken was cancelled."

"He went home to London while Audrey and I went to live with Mr & Mrs Latham."

William J Latham and his wife lived in the last house on the left as you leave Farleigh heading towards Bristol. He was the author of at least two booklets one of which was entitled "Further Wanderings in Somerset."

Daphne remembers

"Having a bath in their very large bathroom, seeing a button on the wall, pressing it to see what happened and, horror of horrors, Mrs Latham and the maid Gladys came charging in. They'd thought I was drowning."

"I am sure Mr and Mrs Latham found 13 year old me to be a real worry; my 9 year old sister was less trouble but we were a package deal. Eventually we were moved to Oldfield House at the western end of West Town."

Audrey Maureen Angela and Daphne in the Blubell Wood (AC)

This was the house of Bernard Whittard and his daughters who were then aged 6 and 11. I have been fortunate to have been able to speak to Angela and have had written details from Maureen in Australia. Angela showed me a copy of the booklet mentioned above which was inscribed

"To my friend Bernard Whittard with all good wishes. Billy Latham May 4th 1938".

Both Angela and Maureen got on well with Daphne and Audrey. Often they went on walks together on the hills and made dens. In the winter of 1939/40 they were able to slide down Breakneck in the snow. The track on Backwell hill was very steep and they had great fun.

Stella remembers

"Some Saturdays in order to spend a few hours by the sea I would walk to Clevedon and back via Chelvey where in the grounds of the waterworks were the tallest monkey trees I had ever seen whilst watercress could be found in the stream nearby."

Daphne's mother came to Oldfield House twice. The first occasion was in November 1939 when Audrey had appendicitis and the second time in late Spring 1940 to tell them she was going to have a baby. That time she stayed with Mr and Mrs Lott.

After the bombing of Bristol, Daphne's and Audrey's beds were moved down to the nursery where it would be safer. They slept there until November when they moved to Chelvey to be with their mother and young baby. The brother was christened Michael by Mr Urch in Backwell Church; a church Daphne remembers with great affection.

Daphne left the area to return to London in March 1941 (about a week before the first bombs on Oldfield House) to work for the Post Office Savings Bank until she was 18 when she joined the Womens Auxiliary Air Force.

I mentioned earlier Louise's arrival at Mrs Waite's cottage. Louise went on to say of her arrival

"With a six month old baby in the house it was wonderful. Everything was so funny to us. The toilet was outside and from 'our time' it was called 'Along the lane'. Mr Waite kept a ferret in a cage in one part of the building. You can imagine we ran both ways."

"There were no schools organised at first so we helped with the harvest. Picking apples and strawberries we made gluttons of ourselves. So many kids were sick and laying under hedges."

"For some while there was a problem. Boys from a "Borstal" type school were placed at the same village. The people would shun us and blame us for all, when they finally moved these older boys everything changed."

Vera Waite explained that the boys, who came from the Stamford Hill area of North London, were placed with local families but these were not told anything of their guests' past misdemeanours and found out the hard way. The North Hammersmith school used the Badminton halls at Backwell House and West Town House for school. There were 5 or 6 classes in each.

"One day we were walking home from West Town to Farleigh. An aeroplane was flying low and making holes in the centre white line of the road. Ladies were screaming to all of us kids to lay down. No way; we were fascinated and wanted to see it all. It was a 'jerry' plane machine gunning."

Louise remembers being vaccinated in the Village Hall before returning to London. Her sister was a bit of a rebel and not as easy as Louise for Mrs Waite to handle. However their father wanted them back in safety. They returned to a farm on top of Backwell Hill where they worked like prisoners.

"We didn't stay long, my mother demanded that we move. I went back to Mrs Waite, who was now having to look after her mother, and my brother and sister went to different places."

Joyce had problems with the billeting officers but stuck to her guns. She was adamant she and her brother were staying together.

"In the end they put us in a car and took us up through Brockley Combe to a house in Downside. When we got there the lady came out to see what had arrived. Seeing the two of us she said 'Oh I can't take a brother and sister. I can only accommodate one'".

The people opposite, who Joyce got to know later, offered to lend them a camp bed but to no avail and Joyce felt especially hurt when the driver said

"You don't have to bother about them like that. I'll take them back"

and take them back he did, all the way to the Parish Hall. Then someone made a decision to try the Cudmores at Yew Tree Farm off the A38. The children were loaded into a car and taken all the way over the hill again to stop outside the farm where

"Three huge dogs came barking round the car and these two elderly people came walking across from the cowsheds carrying the milk. It was evening by then.

We went in; no electric, no water, no bathroom. It was really quite primitive: Mr and Mrs Cudmore looked us over and signed the papers and took us in. They were very nice. I was there until the following July, my brother Maurice stayed nearly three years."

"Mrs Cudmore insisted we bathed before we went to bed. We were not altogether surprised to find it was in a tin bath in front of the fire. After that we were led up to bed by candlelight. My room had a four poster bed. It was very eerie the way the shadows played on the wall. We were both homesick but next morning when I awoke the sun was shining and I looked down on the ducks in the duck pond and then all round the countryside - things didn't seem too bad."

"At the time war was declared on the Sunday we were walking down Potters Hill to post a card to our parents to tell them where we were. I wrote FELTON in capital letters as I knew they would be worried if they thought we were at Filton."

That afternoon she was shown the shortcut to Backwell across the fields and down over Cheston Combe. It poured with rain and they were all drenched by the time they arrived back at the farm.

On Monday 4th September, Joyce said she

"Made the journey to Backwell Playing Fields on my own where the form was to meet to learn of arrangements for school. It wasn't long before things were sorted out. The senior

school was housed in the Badminton Hall at Backwell House and the junior school in the Badminton Hall at West Town House. The "odds and bobs" of brothers and sisters were in the WI and the Parish Halls."

Joyce and Maurice with the Cudmores (JH)

"Lots of school equipment came with us, as did quite a few of the staff and their wives and families, and before long we were fairly well settled."

"In spite of the distance to school and back every day (about 4 miles cross country) we remained at Yew Tree Farm until we returned home."

Joyce took typewriting lessons which Stella remembers took place in Mr Robinson's library and which were always held after normal school hours. Joyce mentions the journey home across the dark fields as being hair raising. On other occasions she remembers waltzing along the top of Backwell Hill to the tune of Flanagan and Allen's Umbrella Song with her friend who was billeted at Cater Farm. When going to school she always set off in wellington boots as the grass was always wet.

"I would change into shoes at the Ridout's cottage on Backwell Hill and leave the wellingtons in the lodge in the garden."

Joyce's brother was a little tearaway who used to alter the school clock causing the teacher to apologise for being late. Joyce used to stop his pocket money. She also used to worry when

"My brother used to take the horse and cart into Bedminster to the corn merchants and came back loaded up. If mum had known he was going down that road she would have had a fit."

Maurice Coyle at Yew Tree Farm (JH)

Being so far from Backwell, Joyce did not have many friends in that area apart from school friends. One she made at Felton was the daughter of Mr and Mrs Franks of Catch Farm who is now married to Fred Patch.

While Joyce was at Yew Tree Farm, Mr Cudmore kept an eye on the boys who used to come. He wouldn't let her out with just anybody but Dennis Horler was allowed to take her to dances at the Village Hall.

When Joyce went back to London she wrote to Dennis but did not get an answer. Then they had a bomb drop in their garden in London. Even that had a humorous side to it.

"Mum would never go to a shelter. Normally we would go downstairs but on this particular night I was giving mum a beauty treatment when the siren went. We stayed upstairs and I had just removed most of a layer of cold cream when there was a terrific explosion. Everything shook and soot came out of the fireplace and stuck everywhere including her face."

"There was an old lady of 80 downstairs and mum's first thought was for her. The house was a shambles but nobody was hurt. There was a rest centre down the road so mum grabbed her hat and took the old lady to the centre. She was concerned

when she came back that everyone grinned when they saw her. It wasn't surprising as not only did she have soot all over her face but she had her hat on back to front."

Joyce's mother asked her to go to Bristol to see if she could find accommodation. She came to Bristol and caught a bus to Felton. Dennis was in his house and saw her get off the bus. He said to his parents "she has come back" and came out to meet her.

"What's all the fuss" I said to him.

"You are pleased to see me now but you couldn't be bothered to write could you?"

"It turned out he had written but I hadn't got his letter. If it hadn't been for the bomb maybe I wouldn't have come back in such a hurry."

Joyce and Dennis married shortly after the end of the war and still live in Felton.

CHAPTER 5

SCHOOL

A year before the war started Wraxall boys school closed and the girls school became mixed infants and juniors with Mrs Cowles the headteacher. In 1939 there was a school at Tickenham, another at Backwell and two at Nailsea. In addition there were two private schools in Nailsea. There may well have been others but no details have been forthcoming from my enquiries.

Older pupils from Wraxall had to make their way to 'Nailsea Senior Parochial School' usually known as Old Church because of its proximity to Holy Trinity Church which is still known to many as Old Church.

Phyllis Rew remembers Mr Gowar the headmaster telling newcomers to the School that he had not used a cane on anyone for a very long time and he didn't want to start now.

Olive Branson was one of the teachers and remembers being concerned about the infants in her class. Many came from West End and brought with them their lunch as there were no school dinners at that time. Some had even had to help with the milking before coming to school.

> *"I used to keep a saucepan on the stove so that I could heat the milk."*

Christchurch School (now Four Oaks) in Silver Street had as its headteacher Miss Morris and many of the comments about the school in this chapter come from the school log book she kept (referred to as CSL). The details were extracted for me by Christine Milton who was the school's headteacher up to a few years ago.

Leaving Nailsea by Bucklands Batch one of the private schools was in a house called Meadowlands in what is now Bucklands Drive. The other school called the Farm School was set up by Janet Barton with her mother and an aunt. Pupils were taken from the start of the war. The first classes were held in a wooden bungalow on Scotch Horn but for reasons explained later the school moved first to St Leonards, a house on the Batch, and finally across the road to take over Meadowlands. Janet Barton has been kind enough to supply much information and many photographs some of which are reproduced in this chapter.

In Backwell there was the one school near the church with Mr Branch as Headteacher and the Fairfield School with Miss Lambert as Headmistress. Miss French also taught there.

1939 was to bring many changes.

> *"1st September 1939. We received notice of the evacuation of London and instruction to prepare for the evacuation in LEA Schools" (CSL)*

As has been described earlier the opening weekend of the war brought the children of North Hammersmith Central School to Backwell and those of Wornington Road LCC School to Nailsea. Most of these were to be long term residents of the area. In addition there were younger brothers and sisters and many mums, expectant mothers and babies. They came at the outset but many returned home after a short time.

Isobel Robinson recorded in her Backwell Local Notes (hereafter referred to as BLN).

> *"5th September 1939 - Poor Backwell! London mothers, children and babies have been evacuated and about 500 have come here. The Parish Hall and the WI Hut have been the Receiving Centres and those concerned with the arrangements have worked nobly. How to continue the education of the children will be a most difficult problem."*

From 4th to 18th September Christ Church School was closed while

> *"The teachers and children of Wornington Road School, North Kensington have used the premises as a meeting place whilst we are working to settle numbers, accommodation etc."(CSL)*

I have already explained how the accommodation problems in Backwell were resolved; this left the Backwell children the use of their own school.

Another solution had to be adopted in Nailsea

> *"18th September 1939 - We start school at 8 am for a four hour session closing at noon. The London teachers and children then occupy the premises from 12.15 pm to 4.15 pm." (CSL)*

This solution overlooked the problems of the parents who were also looking after evacuees as it allowed no time for lunch. From 9th October the hours were changed to 8.15 am to 12.15 pm and 12.45 pm to 4.45 pm. Just enough time to feed a native and an evacuee!

Old Church School had made use of a large room at the Butchers Arms for cookery lessons before the war and continued to do so. It was a five minute walk if you hurried, fifteen if you did not. The room was up a flight of stone stairs (with, "a lovely hand rail to slide down until the teacher stopped you doing so"). It was equipped with long wooden tables, various kitchen tools, a sink and two or three paraffin oil stoves.

As part of her initiation into country life, Grace and a small group did a week's course in Butter and Cheese making. This took place in a room at the "George Inn". She still has the notes she took at the time.

Old Church school was also involved in sharing with the LCC school. Use was made of the Brotherhood hall as well as the main school and the room at the Butchers Arms.

Many children had to walk a considerable distance to and from school. Many of the pupils of that time who have given me information speak with fondness of their teachers. My own belief is that insufficient credit has been given in many accounts to the teachers who overcame shortages of equipment and found time not only to teach but to comfort youngsters away from home for the first time. Many of the teachers were young and found themselves 'dumped' in the country, teaching in alien surroundings and taking on responsibilities for the welfare of their pupils that they had never expected and had received only rudimentary training for.

Farm School on the Batch *(JS)*

Children of the Farm School (L – R) Sheila Wyatt & Brian *(JS)*

Thelma Cherry, Stewart Hobbs, Laurie Webster *(JS)*

Claire, Sheila Cherry, Jean *(JS)*

Pam Brake, John, Hugh, Diana *(JS)*

Janet Barton summarised the main events in the early years of the Farm School.

"While we were at Scotch Horn we made the furniture for the school but could find no suitable place for shelter. We were offered the use of a cellar at the Royal Oak but this was found to be wet and if used meant sheltering amid a lot of glass."

"We began to get too many children and with the problems over finding a suitable shelter we made the decision to move the school to our house St Leonards on the Batch."

"Many of the children are still around - Pamela Brake, Pauline Wyatt, Laurie Webster, Thelma, Sheila and Donald Cherry to name but a few. There were a couple of private evacuees, Nigel Watt son of a BBC producer and a boy from the Courtauld family and a Norwegian girl called Tina."

"We held two sessions daily one in the morning and one in the afternoon. My mother cooked the dinners and my aunt, Mrs Bradley who was a teacher, helped with the lessons."

"The first daylight raid came the day after we moved to St Leonards and a bomb fell nearby blowing out our windows. Fortunately nobody was hurt as we had heard the warden blowing her whistle and had got the children inside."

"Numbers continued to mount and then we heard that Miss Woodward who ran a private school at Meadowlands was going to close her school and move to Cornwall. She agreed to sell us the house and we moved there."

Soon after this Janet gave up teaching and went back to London to take an acting course while her aunt continued with the school.

Phyllis remembers

"Besides taking our satchels to school with our books and sandwiches we had to take our gas masks. Very daunting things they were too, but we were taught to put them on correctly.

Under the chin first, breathing in all the time, over the face, straps over the head and check the rubber edges all round the face to see that it was lying flat to the skin and then breathe out - all done in the space of a second or two. The teachers would make sure we did it correctly then we would do a lesson with masks on. Obviously it was a lesson where talking wasn't needed. We also learnt basic first aid and what to do and use in the event of a mustard gas raid which we feared might happen." In addition the pupils had to know what to do and where to go in the event of an air raid warning sounding."

"Those at Old Church School would go to Holy Trinity Church and would sit two in a pew around the walls of the church and dear John Samuel Gower would play hymns on the organ."

At cookery to take shelter meant going down the outside staircase and sheltering in a passage with bottles along each side.

Those at the Brotherhood Hall would line up and the elder children would take a younger one by the hand and would go across the road to take shelter in the cellars of Moorfields House. Access to these was through an outside flap, which normally Mr Gunning (a teacher), would hold open. Inside the cellar the children would be joined by the lady of the house. They often used to entertain themselves by singing rounds, but the suggestion that they sing "London's Burning" on one occasion, did not seem to be welcomed.

Several people commented on relationships with the evacuees; as the war progressed

"We gradually went back to using the school buildings only and by this time we were all happy together, we learnt to speak with a cockney accent, the Londoners picked up some of our language and came to terms with the animals and the peace of the countryside."

Don Baker remembers

"There was a certain amount of rivalry between the locals and the evacuees. There was the odd fight but generally we got on fairly well and were able to teach each other a thing or two."

Another view was

"They spoke a different language, were unruly, self opinionated and not very well dressed."

Some complained that the evacuees were dirty and had 'nits' in their hair. At that time it was a common complaint and there is little doubt that some of the local children were sufferers before "that lot from London" arrived. Certainly one problem was that evacuation took place at the end of the summer holidays. If it had taken place during term time the 'nit nurse' would have had time to have an effect before the children were moved to the country.

Soon after the LCC school arrived in Nailsea Mr Keate the headmaster wrote to Mr Stock the Clerk to the Parish Council asking for

"Three plots, of about 10 perches each, opposite the new council houses ... as we are anxious to arrange out of doors activities for boys over 11 and share the views of Somerset County Council that it would be splendid if the boys could undertake cultivation of some plots of ground."

There were problems in getting in the required number of hours as can be seen from the following

"17th November 1939 Mr Deacon the Somerset Education Officer visited the school with the Vicar to discuss possible improvements to the lavatories and classrooms and the possibility of using the Methodist room for non desk purposes. At present we are doing gardening and a system of homework in the upper classes to make up the necessary 5¼ hours of lessons per day." (CSL)

I was told one story that rather humorously demonstrates the problems some young teachers met. Two had come down with the LCC school, they were young, female, and had been put in lodgings in Station Road with two elderly ladies. The elderly ladies bedtimes were 9pm and the two teachers were expected to do the same. No wonder that when they heard two evacuees were returning to London early in 1940 they rushed round to seek a new less restrictive billet. Sanctuary was given and the curfew lifted.

The Christchurch School Log gives us a good idea of events during the first four or five months of 1940. There are details of sharing whereby Standard I and the infants use the Methodist School room and Standards II III and IV use the Royal Oak Clubroom from 1.30 to 3.30 each day while they all use the school from 9-12 each day. This was changed so that every other week they use the Halls from 9-11 am and their own school from 1.30 to 4.30 pm.

The winter of 1940 was one of the worst in living memory and the record shows that on

"11th January - attendance is poor."

A month later His Majesty's Inspector of Schools came and on 12th April there is a note

"3 pupils pass the scholarship."

Further changes to the sharing arrangements took place on 7th May 1940 owing to the LCC School Junior class moving to the Parochial School.

"Standards III and IV will be able to use their own class-room all day and need not remove to the Royal Oak

Clubroom."

The Whitsuntide holiday was cancelled because of the seriousness of the war news and the school log continues its commentary on local events.

"4th July 1940 - An air raid warning delayed everyone's arrival. Registers marked late."

"8th July 1940 - The windows of the middle classroom have been fitted with frames of wire netting to lesson the danger of flying glass and splinters."

"The London School now keeps entirely to the Wesleyan School Room except that they use the school yard for recreation and PT. This has meant for the time being our own school has returned to normal conditions. The Royal Oak Clubroom is no longer being used by us."

"19th July 1940 - An air raid warning was given just at the end of afternoon school so we remained in the building until 5.20 pm".

"3rd September 1940 - All the school windows have been treated with a cellophane preparation to try to lessen any danger from flying glass."

"Two brick walls 6 feet high have been built outside the two outer school doors which lead directly to classrooms to check any flying shrapnel."(CSL)

So 1940 passed and we arrived at the start of a new year. People were leaving Bristol and while there was not room in the nearby villages for groups to be evacuated places like Nailsea and no doubt the other villages took in a few.

Because of the Blackout making the mornings very dark the school hours were changed to 9.30 - 12.30 and 1.45 - to 3.45 until spring.

In February 1941 the log book records that the total number of pupils is now 161 with 20 more Bristolian children admitted. Inoculation against diphtheria was given to 600 children. On the 17th March as has already been mentioned it recorded the heavy raid of the night before and few children arriving at school. In May it is noted that 6 children gain free places at Grammar Schools.

"26th June 1941 - The Whitsuntide holiday has been delayed for two weeks so that the children may work more usefully in the hay fields."

"3rd October 1941 - A week's closure is to facilitate children helping with the root crop harvest. New offices are completed 8 WC's for girls and infants; 1 for teachers, 2 WC's for boys and 2 urinals, 1 for older boys, 1 for younger."

There are few later entries which are particularly pertinent to the effects of the war on the school and it must be remembered that the log book related only to the Nailsea school not the London school sharing the premises. However the following give an indication of what went on.

In summer 1942 the school was open for the holiday month for any child whose parents were on war work. The parents have to sign a form to allow their children to attend. Twenty six out of 147 apply. Each week a different teacher helps Miss Morris who works the whole period.

February 1944 shows a familiar problem too few teachers or too many pupils. Numbers are down to 100 but Miss Morris has only one teacher to assist her between February and May in which month a new appointment can be made.

January 1945 brings another bad winter. There are heavy falls of snow - all lavatories and cisterns frozen on 31st January so school is closed.

On 19th April two clerks from the County Architects office come to make a few measurements for some vague purpose while on 1st May a new cleaner is appointed. This happened after Miss Morris had herself spent four days giving the school a thorough clean helped by the other teacher(s).

The evacuees were told in May 1945 that they could return home and by summer the schools would return to local use.

The era can be rounded off with two entries from Miss Morris's logbook.

"2nd July 1945 - Today I have admitted 15 children who for varying periods have attended the Wornington Road Evacuee School held at the Village Institute. All the evacuees wishing to return to London were taken back on June 24th and the school closed on June 29th."

"14th July 1945 - The Head Teacher (Miss Morris) concluded the part time course at Bristol University and received her certificate."

The school was to reopen on 3rd September but during the holiday Victory over Japan was announced. The whole country had two days holiday so the start of the new term was delayed to 5th September.

CHAPTER 6

THE STRANGERS

The War brought many strangers to the Villages besides the evacuees and this chapter tells some of their stories and how they affected the lives of the Villagers.

Our own troops were at Brockley before 1941 where they used the Church for Sunday Parades. In Nailsea, British troops were also in the Drill Hall and opposite in tents in Nailsea Park and I believe the RAMC took over the Village Institute. Some people told me that they saw wounded soldiers in the village but the building was released to the village early in 1940.

On 14th December 1939 the Clerk to the Parish Council read a letter from Mr R C Tanner asking

"If the Council approves that a letter be sent to the appropriate authority asking that the Institute be released for use by the village as it is the only place that any form of entertainment can be held."

It was certainly in use by the village again in July 1940 when a meeting was held to discuss an appeal for scrap iron and the production of vegetables.

Our own troops manned the guns on Backwell Hill and at Markham and other places along the Channel. Searchlights were at West End and at Cadbury Camp and balloons at Ashton Park and along the Channel and over the docks at Avonmouth.

Betty May, was in the WAAF and was stationed at Gordano House, Easton in Gordano. She was in A Flight attached to 927 Squadron, Stoke Bishop, attached to 11 Balloon Centre, Pucklechurch.

There were 6 balloon sites in the area

1) Mushroom Farm
2) On the Ack Ack site
3) Piggery

} Sheephouse Lane, all covering entrance to Avonmouth Docks

4) Portbury
5) Portbury Marshes
6) Pill on the banks of the River Avon

Coloured American troops moved into the huts at Nailsea Park and also into a camp they built at Brockley alongside what is now the A370 (on the right hand side of the road as you travel from West Town towards Weston and before you reach the crossroads at Brockley). The police occasionally had to remove prostitutes from this camp. Apparently they came out from Bristol by bus.

At that time the American forces were not integrated and the locals found there was a certain amount of antipathy between the coloured troops and white troops.

"The white troops who brought rubbish from the hospital to tip in the quarry used to drive back up Station Road and then turn down Nailsea Park just to antagonise the coloured troops."

"The coloured troops used the Lord Nelson and one night there was a fight when a white girl came in with a black soldier. Apparently a white officer took offence."

Mary Stephenson remembers one incident on the green outside the Queens Head

"The black and white troops fought like the very devil. Old Hosey, the policeman, stepped between them. The American Police came down with guns."

"I can remember seeing an American laying down on Parsons corner with a rifle or machine gun on a tripod and another by the old post office."

It seems the reaction of many locals who met coloured troops for the first time was favourable. Jenny Wakeham remembers that her father used to entertain both black and white Americans and that the cook from the camp in Nailsea Park used to bring doughnuts for both her and her sister.

There were many American troops and trucks on the Mendips and for some considerable time it was necessary to have a pass to get into the area.

There was another camp for coloured American troops on the Failand - Bristol road.

Norman Baker was on duty at Flax Bourton Station one night probably in 1943 when three trains full of coloured American Troops arrived at 1.30 am, 3.30 am and 5.30 am. White Americans drove lorries to take them to 60 acres near the Failand Inn.

Norman worked in the signal box where there were three others named Parrish, Childe and Parson. Mr Childe walked there each day from Backwell and stayed on until he was 70.

One night the 9.28 pm train from Nailsea was held just outside Flax Bourton in the cutting. The 9pm Salisbury mail received a direct hit as it pulled out of Bristol and the enemy activity meant that it was too dangerous to allow the Nailsea train into Bristol. It finally got there at 6.30 am.

On another occasion the signalman on duty at FB signal box looked outside and saw a pair of eyes looking at him

"He looked more closely and saw that it was an enormous coloured American with nothing on. He open the door and said you had better come up here. He came in and had a cup of tea while the signalman phoned via the control for someone to come to fetch him."

Apparently this soldier had gone mad and had escaped from

his restraints.

"I couldn't leave him out there or otherwise I would have had to stop the trains!"

White American troops were stationed at Tyntesfield and at Ashton Court and in Ashton Park. It is also said that they were at Brockley. Those at Tyntesfield were members of the 74th(US) General Hospital under Colonel H I Jeperson although there may have been a different unit there earlier. Many of the local people helped at the Hospital. Mrs Stokes remembers working voluntarily for the American Red Cross with the injured soldiers writing letters home and reading letters to them.

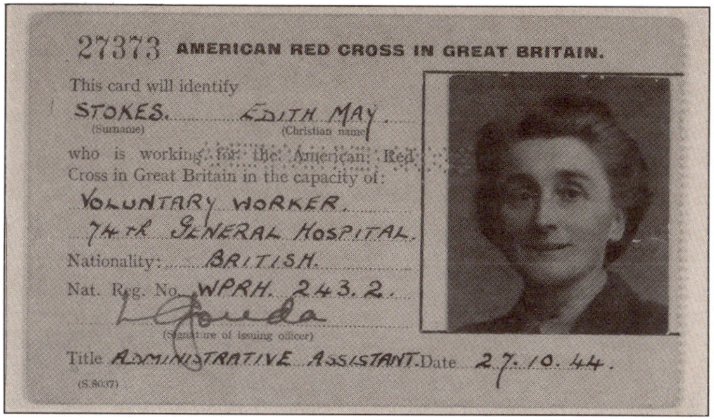

Tyntesfield Hospital ID card *(ES)*

When the Americans left they put on a party to reward the many helpers.

When the US forces moved into Ashton Court Park balloons were placed in Leigh Woods, Ashton Park near the pitch and putt course and in the field at the end of the Long Ashton by-pass. There was also a runway for light aircraft near Beggar Bush Lane I am told.

Other strangers to the area were Prisoners of War (POWs) and there is some confusion about where they were. There was a camp between Cleeve and Yatton. Some say there were Germans at the camp previously used by the Americans at Brockley others equally adamant say there were not. The strength of the 'evidence' seems to point to German POW's being somewhere near the Brockley crossroads camp if they were not in the House or the camp. As with all other parts of the book the author would welcome information confirming or denying statements made.

Prisoners were allowed out to help on farms. Some came from a camp at Failand where they made toys to barter with the locals. Because food was short they were sometimes guilty of stealing food from the locals.

Those that raided a Failand farm and stole a couple of turkeys (being kept for Christmas 1944) left a trail of feathers up Green Lane to the camp.

I have been told that Italian POW's were kept in the camp at Failand after the black Americans had moved out.

Mary Stephenson remembers two German POW's Georg and Kurt coming from a camp opposite Greens garage on the Failand road.

Janet remembers one day exercising her dog and seeing a very fair chap running from behind some bushes, looking scared. He then 'vanished'. At the time she wondered it it was a POW working on Fry's Farm.

There is one rather funny story (but is it true?) about an escaped German prisoner that might well tie in with the one Janet saw.

A suspicious looking character was seen in Nailsea village near Hewetts corner. Someone dashed round to the policeman's house in Station Road and the policeman came round in civies. He agreed that it looked like an escaped prisoner and said to the local men 'keep an eye on him while I go and put my uniform on.'

Strangers also dropped in from the sky unhappily often with fatal results.

Very early in the war a Hurricane landed in an orchard belonging to Manor Farm (Capt. Ridge) knocking down a few trees but otherwise doing little damage. The pilot, a Pole, made his way to Midgell Farm where he had some problems with the language barrier but eventually was able to sort things out.

Norman Baker saw the plane come down as did Clifford Kortright

"I was milking at Brockley Elm Farm in the morning and heard it whistling down and heard him hit the trees. I carried on milking. Before I had finished Capt Ridge and two members of CD arrived and asked if I had seen or heard it or knew where it was. I was able to tell them and they went down and found it."

"About three days later the RAF brought a low loader and I helped to guide it in. The plane was about 100 yards from the road behind where the cattery is now."

It is interesting to see the confusion caused by different witnesses making different judgements of the site of the landing. This information comes from SRO at Taunton (ref CD/GEN/3/26).

"25.8.1940 11.40 to Bristol. Aeroplane down between Chelvey Waterworks and Brockley Church. AO gone to

investigate."

"25.8.1940 12.55 Plane down is a Hurricane Fighter - Police on Guard. Pilot has notified his HQ. Site is a corner of an orchard belonging to Mr Denning on W side of road leading from Brockley Combe X roads to Chelvey 1500 yds NW of H11."

"27.8.1940 22.48 From Nailsea Believed plane down at Flax Bourton. Subsequently established that it was SOM2 of 25.8 Polish pilot."

"28.8.1940 SOM4 from Mr Hall British Hurricane plane came down with Polish pilot midway between St Bridgets Church, Chelvey and Brockley Court in a field 200 yards SSW of Brickyard wood. This was originally reported as falling between Belmont Hill and Flax Bourton Railway Station."

About a month later the CD records (see appendix) give details of bombs dropped on Nailsea, and refers to

"25.9.1940 Enemy plane down 11.50 am Racecourse Farm."

This was the Heinkel He 111 commanded by Oberleutnant G Weigel who with his crew became the first invaders of this part of Somerset.

Another of the contributors to this book was at Porlock on 27th September 1940 when she saw Helmut Ackenhausen crash land his Junkers Ju 88 on Porlock Beach to avoid being shot out of the sky.

On the 22nd February 1941, Vernon Ridley was riding his bicycle home from Bristol and seems to remember flakes of snow falling. When he was near to the Failand Inn

"I saw one in trouble ... it was a German."

It was another Heinkel 111 which came down on the mud flats at Portbury; the Pilot Berndt Rusche survived but the remainder of the crew were killed.

Early in 1942 on 8th February a Hurricane piloted by Sgt J R Keith of the RCAF crashed at Naish Farm killing the pilot.

Much later in the year on 17th December an Airspeed Oxford

"Came from the direction of Wraxall flying low up the valley. It didn't sound as if it was in trouble but it just missed Old Church and then caught the lower cable of the electric supplies near to a pylon in the second field to the west of Engine Lane."

Vernon recalls that he and his father were the first ones there

"It was an awful mess .... there was one body in the hedge. One of the dead did not appear to be a member of the aircrew. We thought he had hitched a lift. There was a bicycle on board."

Vernon's father was the local undertaker and was the official layer out of bodies killed due to the war. The place he used was a small room adjacent to the Royal Oak. It was used until quite recently for hairdressing.

On 5th August 1943 an Airspeed Oxford crashed on Chelvey Batch killing both crew members.

This was followed by another crash near Wraxall House on 16th December 1943 recorded by the CD.

"Spitfire Mark IV crashed 1/4 mile SSW of Wraxall Church. Map ref 931 926 complete wreck."

"Pilot baled out, parachute failed to open."

Mrs Coker was walking from her home in Tower House Lane to Nailsea and had just entered the main road when the plane swept low across the road and crashed some distance to her left. Many workers from 'Coates' came running down the road.

Stewart Freeman is sure he knows where the plane had crashed.

The South West Aircraft Recovery Group carried out several searches to find the site and it was only at the end of 1989 they felt sure they had found it. However, as one mystery was solved another arose. They had spoken to more witnesses than I was able, in preparing this book, and their leader is almost sure that the stories told to them relate to two different incidents and to two, not one, aircraft which crashed at different times in the same area. One was taken away probably fairly intact. The other was a complete wreck. The author would appreciate details of the plane taken away nearly whole.

The Spitfire that crashed apparently ran out of fuel on a flight from Gibraltar to RAF Benson. The photographic version was designated PR IV and carried up to 133 gallons of fuel giving it a greatly extended range and caused it to be nick named 'the flying bowser'. It was very difficult to control for about an hour after take-off due to the excessive weight of fuel but this one appears to have run out of fuel.

It is not altogether surprising that there were accidents in the area. Despite the attacks early in the war it became fairly safe for training pilots. They had to practice low flying and they did so in the area unfortunately sometimes with fatal results. Eric McEwen-Smith remembers the humorous side of one incident

"They used to train pilots and they would come along about 10 feet off the ground and at times would touch their wheels on the ground.

"Old Chummy Wilmott and I were cutting out some hay down on the Tickenham Moors to bring it up to Hales Farm. Chummy had not seen these planes doing that. He was on top of the mow and I said 'Look out Chummy he's coming'. There was this ruddy plane coming straight at him."

"Chummy chucked the hay knife on the ground and slipped

down the mow and the plane went 'whoosh' straight over the top. I believe the pilot saw Chummy on the top and did it on purpose. Chummy was an oldish man but, by god, he shifted off there. He didn't bother about the ladder or anything else."

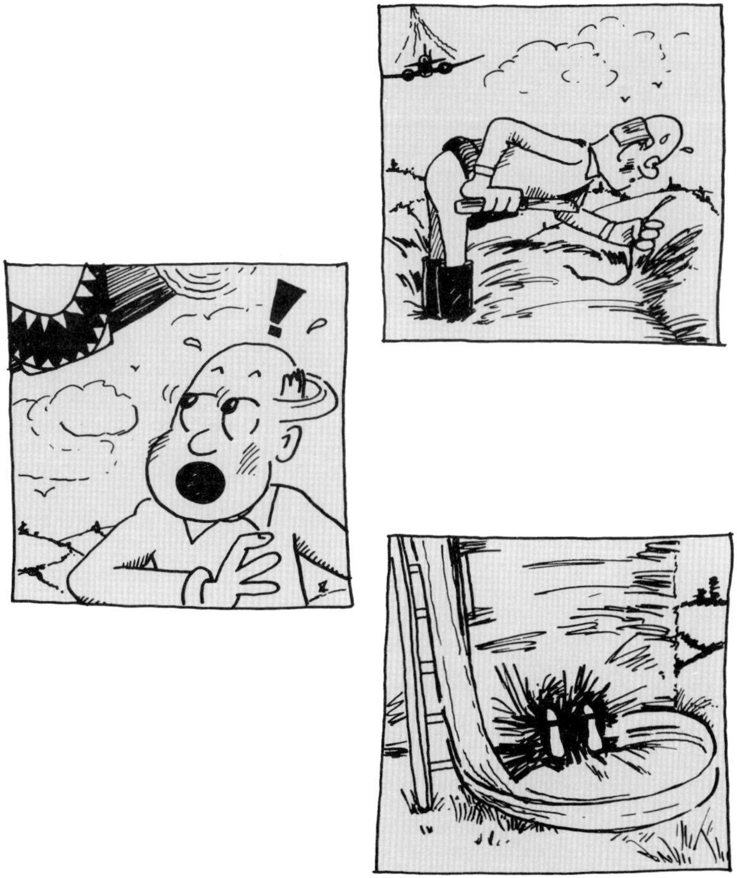

The other strangers include the official evacuees who have already been represented in these pages, those who moved here because of their work or for reasons of safety. The wounded, both physically and mentally, who were housed at Barrow Hospital and Wraxall Court. (Here although it was not used in this war let me mention Commander Evans who offered the use of part of Nailsea Court for a hospital as he did with more success in the first war). The strangers also include those who came to work on the land.

The Ministry of Agriculture took to itself very wide powers and required the maximum use be made of the land. If this was not done a farmer could be, and frequently was, dispossessed of his land for bad husbandry. As with all such sweeping powers they were sometimes abused. Farmers if they were any good knew what their land could produce and were inclined to ignore instructions from someone sitting behind a desk if those instructions were, in the farmer's view, wrong.

Mary Stephenson came from Bootle to learn her trade in the Women's Land Army at Steambow Farm, Pilton. This was a farm that had been taken over and had been open for a month to provide training. When she arrived she found POW's and conscientious objectors also being trained.

"I was sent to Lady Wraxall at Tyntesfield. I was met at Flax Bourton Station by a chauffeur in livery, peaked cap, gauntlet gloves, pouchy trousers, double breasted coat. He looked absolutely fantastic and drove me to the farm where I was to work for Mr and Mrs Brimble. Mr Brimble was Lady Wraxall's bailiff having taken over from Ernest Wyatt who had died."

"Home Farm supplied milk, eggs and poultry to the Big House. With the two boys at Eton when I arrived Lady Wraxall took a very active interest in the farm."

"It was a very modern farm for its time and had a milking machine; I was delighted because I wasn't very good at milking. She kept a pedigree herd of shorthorns; they were lovely. They were dual purpose annuals good for beef and good for milk. When being milked they had individual attention, certain cows being milked by hand."

"We had sows and our own boar pigs and bred our own little pigs. The sows were kept in a Danish type piggery - quite modern boxes with doors that opened into alley ways which could be shut off as could the pen."

"Haymaking and harvesting were very different to what it is today."

Although it was much more of a manual operation most of it was done by land girls. Some of it was very heavy work.

"The corn went into 2¼ cwt (115kg) sacks and I used to be able to carry a sack and tip it into a bin. As long as I had two ears to hold I could get it onto my back."

"Dairy feed came in 1¼ cwt (63kg) sacks. I used to help unload the lorries."

Lady Wraxall used to go to Scotland to buy Highland cattle,

Belted Galloways

"All cows had horns in those days. These cattle would come down by lorry and we would pen them all the winter. We threw in clean straw every day but they were never cleaned out. By the time spring came and they went to market the muck had to be cleaned out. It was deep and solid as a rock. With Teddy the evacuee at the farm, I had to cut round with a hay knife and pull it with a fork."

"Oh I can remember now the joy when you actually hit the bottom and you felt the stone. It was ever such hard work. We used to work very hard. I was fed well but I was lucky because I was in a good farm. It was a great change of life because suddenly you were in a very quiet place. Mr and Mrs Brimble went to bed about 8.30 - 9 pm."

"Milk had to be ready in the morning - it went to a retailer called James, at Long Ashton."

"When he got to Tyntesfield he would bottle up more milk - churns were sometimes 10, 12 or 17 gallons. The milk had to be ready for him otherwise he got a bit narky."

"I was the dairy maid and I used to do all the washing up and get the milk ready. There were 10 stone steps from the floor of the dairy to the churn stand at the top. He wouldn't carry the churns up so unless I got someone to do it for me I had to do it myself. The churn itself weighed about 20 lbs and the milk it contained about 170 lbs."

The milk was bottled using an adapter and a capper and sometimes Mary was asked to do this as well.

Tyntesfield also kept sheep and these had to be examined each day removing maggots and bathing feet as necessary. Where there was particularly trouble with maggots the wool was trimmed off and Stockholm Tar put on the bare flesh. Where tails were to be removed they were cut off, rubber bands were not used at Tyntesfield.

Mary remembers the roar of aero engines when she was working near the top road (the Clevedon-Bristol road). They were tested in a quarry a short distance down Portbury Lane. She also mentioned the Doreen Hut which continued in use for dances even after the war. The hut was a wooden chalet type building in a copse on the north of the Wraxall-Bristol road just before the Jubilee Cottages. It was built by Lord Wraxall for the Villagers to use as a village hall for plays and dances. It was named after Miss Doreen Gibbs.

When Mary arrived at Tyntesfield, the American Hospital had already been built and the longest holly hedge in England had been breached to provide access to the hospital. It was supposed to be the largest American Hospital in North Europe. General Eisenhower is believed to have visited the hospital. (In the course of writing this book I have failed to trace a single photograph that gives any impression of the hospital).

The Yanks used to wander all over Tyntesfield wearing red dressing gowns.

"They would come to give us candy bars. One even brought Mrs Brimble a dressing gown. They were very generous. Nearly all were white - there were very few coloured. In fact I cannot remember any walking wounded who were black."

"We used to use the Battleaxes and never saw any black Americans there. White walking wounded would come there as they got better."

After her time at Tyntesfield, Mary went to a farm at Clevedon. Eventually she married Eric, took a great interest in local government and eventually became Chairman of Woodspring District Council. She and her husband now live in Tickenham.

CHAPTER 7

VICTORY

Most contributors had memories of the day and the parties which took place shortly after.

In Nailsea, Olive Branson was getting ready to take Peter to a celebration in Backwell when her husband, who she thought was in Burma, walked in.

In Cleeve a party was held on the forecourt of the garage which has recently been demolished.

Backwell held one in the Fairfield using the hut abandoned by the searchlight unit that had been stationed there.

Victory Party Chapel Alley *(JC)*

Nailsea had major celebrations and bonfires next to Dr Naomi Bown's house (near the corner of High Street and Nailsea Park) on the Martyrs field and also outside the New Inn at West End and there were street parties in several places including Chapel Alley.

It has not been possible to establish clearly which were the VE celebrations and which were VJ day. Maybe it is because of the state of the revellers

"What do you remember of the celebrations?"

"Not a lot, I was drunk most of the time. I remember going to the Battleaxes and everybody was high as a kite."

The following comments give a hint of the excitement

"I was at boarding school outside of Hereford in the house owned by Madeleine Carroll the famous film star and her husband; the senior girls put the Union Jack over the door."

"A lighted firework fell in the open box of fireworks at the Martyrs Field bringing the celebration to an end with a big bang."

"We had a lovely time on the Oak front, it's where I first met Vernon."

"We danced around the bonfire in the middle of the road outside the New Inn, at West End, Nailsea (the mark was there for years after). There was community singing. I played the piano accordion - a boy was instructed to stand at my elbow and follow me with a full pint of cider all the time - which duty he did most satisfactorily. That binge lasted three days because I went over to Tickenham, was there for a day and then went to Grove Farm Backwell, where a guy of Hitler was burnt."

Nailsea Parish Council contributed towards the celebrations as, I suspect, did the other Village Councils.

In Nailsea VJ night was remembered for the fire at Heath Minerals which flared up about 11.30 pm. Norman Baker helped fight this fire and remembers

"Poor old Reg Baker was overcome by smoke. He fell out of the ladder and had to be taken to hospital."

"I didn't get home until about 3.30 am."

Those who lived in Wraxall were given a welcome home party soon after demob.

Homecoming, Wraxall (for names see Appendix) *(EC)*

And so the story of the four villages in wartime ends.

Although war is sad it is tinged with many happy memories - new friends made, new jobs learnt, a taste of the country. It is something those who lived through it will never forget. Sadly these people are getting fewer and fewer but it is right that their memories should live on; it is also right that we should understand what they went through and how life went on over 40 years ago.

APPENDIX

Homecoming, Wraxall

Back Row:
1. , 2. John Frappel, 3. Hatten, 4. Harold Clark, 5. Reg Clark, 6. Bob Davies, 7. Roy Coker, 8. Bill Willcox, 9. Bill Elvered, 10. Raymond Davis (Charlie), 11. Alf Weeks, 12. Herbert Davey, 13. Leslie Clark?, 14. Cyril Davey, 15. , 16. Leslie Clark?, 17. , 18. Stanley Vowles, 19. Jack Parsons.
2nd Row: (from back)
1. Mr. Falcon, 2. Rev. Bromhead, 3. Stanley Frappell, 4. Bob Shipway, 5. Betty Shipway, 6. Donald King (Don's father), 7. Peggy Watkins, 8. Ken Biggins, 9. , 10. , 11. Evelyn Russell, 12. Mary Wyatt, 13. (In front of L. Clark) Ivor Vowles, 14. Sid Vowles, 15. David Mitchell, 16. John Orchard, 17. , 18. , 19. Miss Briggs (Elizabeth), 20. , 21. (Pipe) Arthur Petty.
Front Row:
1. Mr. E. Price, 2. Mr. Coates, 3. Mr. Subner, 4. Rev. Briggs, 5. Mr. Vowles, 6. Mr. Isles, 7. Mrs. Biggins, 8. Mrs. J. Mitchell, 9. Mr. Orchard.

Much of the information in the chapter "Villages under Attack" not obtained from the Villagers together with the following details were obtained from items at Taunton Records Office filed under the references CD/CL/1&2 CD/GEN/3/26,27,28 and 29. No attempt was made to record raids on Long Ashton or Bristol and selective use only was made of details relating to parishes around the four villages.

The "Filton" Raid 25th September 1940 "between 11.35 am and 12.23 pm .... 9 HE and 2 petrol bombs and incendiaries fall and explode in Nailsea
3 in Trendlewood field
2 in Little Nailsea
1 at East End House Nowhere
1 at East End Farm
1 at Greenacres
1 at White Oak
1 incendiary at East End Farm
1 Petrol bomb at East End Farm
1 Petrol bomb at White Oak.
No damage or casualties.
One Ambulance to Charlton House Top Gate Failand - one German airman suffering from leg fractures to Clevedon Hospital. 4 parachutes. 1 UXB 50 yds from The Cottage, Wraxall.
Enemy plane down at 11.50 am Racecourse Farm. 5 UXB's there also 4HE and 2 Petrol bombs in field of Failand Lodge Farm.
5 HE and 1 petrol bomb in field and garden, Home Farm Tyntesfield. 2 cottages, Farm House and outbuilding badly damaged. Water main fractured - cut off water to Tyntesfield House."

19th November 1940*
"Revised sum of occurrences.

3 HE	One in field of Brown Rock Farm, Tickenham, two in Clapton Wood, Cadbury Camp Lane
1 UXB	100 yards Nailsea side of Tickenham Church and about 20 yards from the Causeway. Road Closed.
1 HE	400 yards NNW of HT pylon near Kings Hill Farm 1 HE 26 yards ditto (sic)
1 HE	200 yards N of Nailsea House
1 HE	at rear of house in Church Lane
1 HE	at rear of house occ by Mrs Hughes, St Marys Grove, SE of School, SW of Rectory and Holy Trinity Church. Slight damage to windows and to roof.
3 HE	on right (or maybe rear) of Youngwood Farm - no casualties
1 HE	directly south of above in open field 1 HE at base of embankment GWR directly south of the above and ¼ mile from station.

*(Although the entry is dated 19.11.1940 I believe these all relate to incidents of 17/18.11.40. PW)

4/5th January 1941

22.30	Tickenham Hill - Many incendiaries trees burnt. 4 Houses hit – extinguished.
22.20	Silver Street, Nailsea - Numerous incendiaries. Nil damage/casualties.
22.29	Tickenham Court Road - 4 HE.
22.45	Nailsea Moor - numerous incendiaries
	Cadbury Lane - 1 HE private road belonging to Dr Gleeny.
	Tickenham - 1 HE plus 1 HE or land mine. Crater of second 60 ft wide, 20 feet deep.
	Barrow Gurney - Naval Hospital 10 HE & 1 UXB, no damage or casualties

16/17th January 1941
Lower Failand – 1 HE & numerous incendiaries, no damage or casualties.
1 person killed (near Long Ashton Golf Club)

22.30 Backwell – 1 HE, 1 UXB doubtful. Fell on Backwell Common Farm in field belonging to Mr Seamane, Dibdens Farm, Backwell just to west of GWR main line.

31st May 1941

0100 1 HE fell in field at Nailsea. Crater 26 feet by 60 feet. 1 cow killed belonging to Miss McMillan of Nailsea.
a) Damage to roof of North Somerset Electric Lighting Co resident engineers house ¼ mile away.
b) Smithfield (sic) Road and surrounding houses damaged and interior and around Congregational Church.

(I presume the reference to Congregational Church was meant to be Christ Church. PW).

16/17th June 1941

Wraxall – 15 HEs fell in line NE to SW all estimated to be 50 kilo starting 270 yards S of the Kennels, Wraxall to 200 yards ENE of Combe Grange 550 yards NW of the railway station.

Casualties – 1 male killed Mr S Austin 1 male injured Mr J Summers 1 woman injured Mrs Austin 5 cows killed; 3 injured (1 destroyed).

Hillcrest – Station Road, Nailsea demolished - no casualties. One bungalow at Nowhere Lodge Lane, 1000 yards SE of Nailsea crossroads. House badly damaged, no damage to electric lines or watermains. One telephone out of action.

Wraxall – In field known as Long Ground, Mr Marshalls Farm approx 400 yards NW of Brook Farm in corner of field near river. No casualties or damage.

28th June 1942

Heavy raid on Weston Super Mare. Red Warning 01.27. The following CD personnel were sent from Clevedon District
2 Ambulances
1 First Aid Party from Backwell
1 First Aid Party from Chapel Hill
2 Sitting case cars
1 Rescue Squad (Tarr and Brown)
1 Rescue Squad from Backwell
Arrived RZ 11 White Hart about 03.53.

29th June 1942

Another heavy raid on Weston Super Mare. Red Warning 01.58. The following CD personnel were sent from Clevedon District.
1 First Aid Party Chapel Hill
1 First Aid Party Yatton
ARP Full time Rescue Squad
Council No (?) Rescue Squad
BRO (Mr Settles) and AO (Mr B C Hall) went with the convoy.
All returned by 20.00
Clevedon Mobile Canteen sent
Backwell Rescue Squad dispatched 18.20 hrs returned 00.15.

NORTH HAMMERSMITH CENTRAL SCHOOL

The school was in a two storey building in Bryony Road, Shepherd's Bush. It opened in 1931 and the buildings were used as a fire station during the war. Among the staff and pupils who moved to Backwell during the war were

STAFF

Mr Jameson – The Headmaster
Mr Hisee – with wife and child(ren) lived in a house owned by one of the Revills
Miss Ayres – Deputy Head
Mr Dinsmore – with his wife who also taught at the school. They had a baby - not sure if born in London or Backwell.
Mr Winterton – French teacher - he left the school possibly to teach in Bristol.

PUPILS who have contributed to this book.
GRACE CHAMPION now living in MELBOURNE, AUSTRALIA
LOUISE COOK now living in ONTARIO, CANADA
JOYCE COYLE now living in FELTON, nr BRISTOL
STELLA CRAFER now living in WICKFORD, ESSEX
DAPHNE WANFORD now living in CHICHESTER, SUSSEX

ACKNOWLEDGEMENTS

Without the help of the people named below this story could not have been told for it is their story.
(*indicates that they were interviewed by the author; the place names shown are where they currently live).

BACKWELL – John Brain; Len Elverd*; Angela Lewis; Rhona Rich; Isobel Robinson (deceased); Janet Saunders*; Vera Waite*.

NAILSEA – Don and Audrey Baker*; Norman and Peggy Baker*; Olive Branson*; Mrs E. Clark; Jack Clement; Mrs E. Coker*; Audrey Fido; Monica and Stewart Freeman*; Margaret Frogley*; Mrs and Mrs Grey; Mrs A. Hall*; Mrs L. Howarth; Phyllis Horman*; Edgar and Nora Hurford; Eileen Johnson*; Clifford Kortright*; Christine Milton; Antonia Mitchell; Violet Murray; Jenny Newton; Ivy Port*; Vernon and Doreen Ridley*; Norman and Thelma Searle*; Mary Shepstone*; Phyllis Stacey*; Leslie and Edith Stokes*; Owen Taylor; Mr and Mrs R. Vance*; Freda Vowles.

AND – Graham Ball FAILAND; Daphne Bingham CHICHESTER; Maureen Chlupac AUSTRALIA; Angela Crutchley* FELTON; Grace Golding AUSTRALIA; Betty Hall BLAGDON; Stella Harbert WICKFORD; Robin Haworth* CLEEVE; Joyce and Dennis Horler* FELTON; David Lawrence PORTBURY; Ray Llewellyn* TYNTESFIELD; Eric and Mary McEwen-Smith* TICKENHAM; Louise O'Quinn CANADA; Cis Weeks WRAXALL; Cyril Willcox WRAXALL

Thanks also to Trevor Bowen for help with interviews and assistance in other ways; David Cains for producing photographs, Phyllis Horman for research and always knowing the right person to check a story with especially about Wraxall and reading the drafts; Norma Knight for advice on the drafts and general advice; Margaret Thomas for similar guidance and Vera Waite for helping me to get the facts on Backwell correct and Dudley Wallis for helping me get more than the first words right and David Sessions for technical advice.

PHOTOGRAPHS

Many people loaned photographs for the project and gave permission for them to be used to illustrate the book. However it has not been possible to use them all. Copies have been deposited in the Nailsea and District Local History Society Archive and the owner's copyright is acknowledged.
We thank:-
Daphne Bingham, Maureen Chlupac, Mrs E. Clark, Jack Clement, Angela Crutchley, Stella Harbert, Joyce and Dennis Horler, Eileen Johnson, Ray Llewellyn, Ivy Port, Vernon and Doreen Ridley, Janet Saunders, Norman and Thelma Searle, Mary Shepstone, Phyllis Stacey, Leslie and Edith Stokes and Cis Weeks.

SUBSCRIBERS

(Other than those whose names are acknowledged elsewhere)
J Woods; Denis Bagshawe; Maurice Coyle; Roger Mitchell; P S Hodson; Adrian and Judith Codrington; Derek Robertson; Norma Knight; Cecile Braide; Tim Leggate; Colin Griffin; Derek Bailey; S F Tripp; Jan Barber; M S Horlick; Mrs S C J Russell; Laurie and Pauline Burbridge; Don Goldney; Mr and Mrs B Dejean; Bertram Gray; Ron Edwards; John Brain; Christine Milton; Owen Taylor; Mrs G K Pease; Hilary Atkinson; Margaret Fleming; J A Stacey; Geoffrey John Taylor; John R Allen; Diane Bennett; Richard Brock; G J Allen; Mr Derek Watson; Mrs Rita Watson; Miss Annie Luxton; Neil and Elizabeth Saddington; W/Comdr B J May; E W Crawford; J F Williamson; John Bedford; A F Stirratt; C A Marsh; Audrey Downing; Ronald Wanford; V J Peckham; David and Anne Chappell; Margaret Stenhouse; John Oman; Mr and Mrs B J Knill; Mr S Knill; Mr and Mrs R Watson; Miss V Knill; Gillian Selwyn; Andrew Elverd; Mrs Jean Weatherburn; Bill Shears; Michael Summers; Brian Port; John Port; Colin Port; Alan Port; Gerald Port; G S Dear; Mrs E Parker; Veronica Fox; Jean L Glasson; Mrs P Harris; Stuart Arthur; Mrs Hilda Whittle; Mrs Kathie Reynolds; Mr G E S Smith; Mr E S Wood; Don and Norah Wright; J F and V B Dean; Mr and Mrs T Bowen; F J Clement; C M Nash; Patricia Ballinger; Audrey Carradine; John A Carradine; S O Phillips; Tony Targett; Michael Tozer AND
Nailsea Library
Avon Libraries and Information Service (Community Leisure Dept County of Avon). Nailsea Town Council.

Peter Wright
6th July 1990